MEDIA
MERGERS

Media Studies Series

America's Schools and the Mass Media,
edited by Everette E. Dennis and Craig L. LaMay

Children and the Media,
edited by Everette E. Dennis and Edward C. Pease

Covering Congress,
edited by Everette E. Dennis and Robert W. Snyder

The Culture of Crime,
edited by Everette E. Dennis and Craig L. LaMay

Higher Education in the Information Age,
edited by Everette E. Dennis and Craig L. LaMay

The Media in Black and White,
edited by Everette E. Dennis and Edward C. Pease

Media and Democracy,
edited by Everette E. Dennis and Robert W. Snyder

Media Mergers,
edited by Nancy J. Woodhull and Robert W. Snyder

Media and Public Life,
edited by Everette E. Dennis and Robert W. Snyder

Publishing Books,
edited by Everette E. Dennis, Craig L. LaMay, and Edward C. Pease

Radio—The Forgotten Medium,
edited by Edward C. Pease and Everette E. Dennis

MEDIA MERGERS

EDITED BY

Nancy J. Woodhull
Robert W. Snyder

Transaction Publishers
New Brunswick (U.S.A.) and London (U.K.)

Copyright © 1998 by Transaction Publishers, New Brunswick, New Jersey 08903. Originally published in the *Media Studies Journal*, Spring/Summer 1996. Copyright © 1996 by The Freedom Forum Media Studies Center and The Freedom Forum.

This book is printed on acid-free paper that meets the American National Standard for Permanence of Paper for Printed Library Materials.

Library of Congress Catalog Number: 97–23197
ISBN: 0–7658–0409–3
Printed in the United States of America

Library of Congress Cataloging-in-Publication Data

Media mergers / edited by Nancy J. Woodhull and Robert W. Snyder.
    p.   cm.—(Media studies series)
    Originally published in the spring/summer 1996 issue of Media studies journal.
    Includes bibliographical references and index.
    ISBN 0–7658–0409–3 (pbk. : alk. paper)
    1. Mass media—Mergers. I. Woodhull, Nancy J. II. Snyder, Robert W., 1955–
III. Series.
P96.M46M43   1997
302.23—dc21
                                                    97–23197
                                                      CIP

Contents

Part I: Point/Counterpoint

A sociologist and media critic views the recent mergers with skepticism.
"Today's deals may weigh on the culture for decades. The potential for harm
is at least as impressive as the potential for good. If the country believed in
the countervailing authority of the government, the recourse would be obvious.
It's time for the sheriff to step in and say, Not so fast."

"It is truly ironic to be assessing the impact of mergers on media competition
just as we are entering what may well prove to be the golden age of competition
in communications industries," argues an investment banker and former
journalist. "Look in almost any direction and you see developments that will
benefit consumers."

Part II: The Imperial Moment

"Many economists will testify that corporate mergers work in the best social
interest—by attracting investments to those enterprises that show the greatest
promise of efficiency and productivity," notes an author and media analyst.
"But is profitability the only proper measure of a firm that deals in the facts
that shape history and the fictions that represent a nation's collective dreams?"

"Are there any certainties in the communications revolution?" asks an author and media critic. "Actually, there are some, and not all of them are comforting."

"The primary rationale for regulation has been the need to compensate for the imbalance of power between huge monopoly suppliers and small technically ignorant users," writes a professor of finance and economics. "In a converged environment with full choice, however, the imbalance will change. This will largely resolve traditional problems of price, quality, security, privacy and content diversity."

Part III: Captains of Communication

"The earlier generation of moguls built empires on both passion and profits," observes a journalist and historian. "In today's generation, however, the passion is fading."

A former newspaper publisher explores the image of the media mogul in American culture. "Whether as movie hero or anti-hero, the anything-to-get-the-story reporter has stood for American journalism's freedom and power, its independence and individuality. But the reporter's boss, the news media owner, has represented a more paradoxical, less appealing icon."

"In the uncertain climate that defines life in communications industries today, experience can be an enemy," according to the chairman and CEO of Playboy Enterprises. "For media industry leaders, one of the keys is a willingness to suspend confidence in your own knowledge."

"The different media industry segments are not a monolith of values just because they have been linked by strategies and corporate charters," observe three media analysts. Indeed, a survey of communications executives reveals differences over vertical integration and creativity.

Part IV: States of Media

"To understand media mergers, you must understand their terminology," say two observers. "Therefore, as a public service, we present our readers with a glossary to help them grasp the true import of these momentous changes in medialand and its vocabulary."

"In a world of mergers and media conglomerates, the really influential meetings are the expensive and exclusive conferences where high-level executives outline their corporate agendas, debate their visions and impress the men who prime the media money pumps on Wall Street," asserts a veteran producer. "Yet for all their importance, these conferences form part of a media world not aggressively covered in the mainstream press."

Moderated by *Alex Jones*
Participants: *Frank A. Bennack Jr., Neil S. Braun, P. Anthony Ridder and Arthur Ochs Sulzberger Jr.*

Part V: The Consequences of Media Empires in the United States

"It is time, high time, that newspaper corporations become subjects of debate and be held accountable for covering the communities they serve," writes a veteran newspaper editor. "Meanwhile, many are managing their newspapers like chain shoe stores, with no sense of being important community institutions with highly important responsibilities to the public."

"In an era of corporate mergers and multibillion-dollar lawsuits, big news needs big business," says a former network news executive turned financial analyst. "At issue is not whether there will be a corporate parent, but the integrity and size of the corporate parent."

"Hollywood is in the midst of another anxious evolution, as studio and independent production companies are swallowed up by huge vertically integrated monoliths," writes an independent producer. "Yet, rather than transform the way movies are made, these mergers are merely going to accelerate a transformation already under way toward greater emphasis on the bottom line, more homogenization of content and less risk taking. "

A former radio news executive reflects: "From where I sit, the future of radio news looks pretty grim. It's been in trouble for a long time, plagued by a combination of federal deregulation, market forces and mergers."

"If media companies continue to merge," a book editor believes, "perhaps they will gain the discipline to restrain their subsidiaries from publishing so much, and force them to focus on those few books around which the mythical Common Reader can commune and discuss."

"Publishers and telecommunications companies may well merge," notes the managing editor of a newsletter on the future of communications and computing technology, "but what they do with their merged talents will be very different from the dystopian, one-way, video-on-demand future that seems to have motivated such mergers before."

Part VI: The Consequences of Media Empires Around the World

"There is no question that the Asian market, specifically the East Asian market, is the place to be for international companies eager to expand sales," according to a journalist in Hong Kong. "However, some of the biggest players in the media business have appeared to underestimate just how difficult it is to operate in this region where governments are notably wary of foreign media influence."

"Central and Eastern Europeans can't just jump into the realm of ideal democratic media," admits a Hungarian media analyst. "They also have to reconcile themselves with the less shiny parts of the media market, including relations with international media conglomerates."

"In the middle of this decade, the comfortable world of Latin American network television has been turned on its head, and nowhere more so than in Brazil," a correspondent from Rio de Janeiro suggests. "Gringo capital, long a cultural taboo and often barred outright by national constitutions, is being openly and eagerly courted from the Rio Grande to Patagonia. Suddenly Latin America is a bowl full of angelfish, and the local species will have to swim hard or risk being swallowed."

"Out of Africa, always something new," observes a South African Broadcasting Corp. producer. "In this case, the new is the growth of a homegrown media conglomerate, M-Net of South Africa, whose presence around the continent is a measure of both the modest state of indigenous media industries and Africa's relationship to international media conglomerates."

Part VII: Books

"We are rushing toward a digital world where hundreds or even thousands of channels of information will be available in a variety of formats," observes a media scholar. "Yet in our euphoria for such a diversity of choice we often neglect to ask, What voice will consumers really have in who is going to program all of those channels?"

Preface

Where are the mergers taking news media, entertainment media and big business? The answers are not entirely clear. The consequences of consolidation vary by media industry, and the evolution of communication technology is so fast that today's truisms can be undone tomorrow.

For now, anyone who wants to understand the mergers will be best served by a healthy dose of skepticism, a search for illuminating facts and a willingness to consider *all* sides of the discussion. The best and the worst possibilities of the mergers have been articulated so loudly that everyone should be on guard against both hyperbole and facile judgments. In that spirit, we offer this collection of essays.

We begin with a point/counterpoint section. "Today's deals may weigh on the culture for decades. The potential for harm is at least as impressive as the potential for good," writes Todd Gitlin, a sociologist and media critic. Steven Rattner, an investment banker who specializes in media mergers and acquisitions, believes that "we are entering what may well prove to be the golden age of competition in communications industries."

Six more sections follow. The essays in "The Imperial Moment" set the context for the age of media mergers. "Captains of Communication" and "States of Media" contain essays on the moguls and their empires; their effects are explored in "The Consequences of Media Empires in the United States" and "The Consequences of Media Empires Around the World." A review essay devoted to recent books on media mergers and communication concludes the volume.

Just as it is impossible to take in a grand vista with a single glance, so it is impossible to understand something as big as the mergers from only one perspective. This book approaches the emergence of media giants from a variety of angles. Our contributors offer many ways of understanding their scale and their significance. Together, they can help us come to more solid judgments about this brave new world of media.

In addition to the writers whose work appears in this volume, we also thank Ken Auletta, Leo Bogart, Richard MacDonald and David Shenk for their advice in planning the collection; Karen Verlaque for her research; and Lisa DeLisle, Jennifer Kelley, Alexis Kim and Nathaniel Daw for their editorial work. Finally, we note that Nancy J. Woodhull, co-editor of this volume when it appeared as an issue of *Media Studies Journal*, passed away April 1, 1997.

THE EDITORS

Introduction

For journalists, the recent surge in media mergers has set off a wave of stories that all hit very close to home. In some cases, the very news organizations they work for have become news—and they have to cover it. More often, the formation of communication conglomerates raises profound questions for reporters' lives and work, for instance:

— What is the best way to cover stories of such scale and complexity?
— Will the new giants broaden both the definition of journalism and the opportunities for journalists to practice their craft?
— What are the prospects for the new partnership of big news, new media and big business?

Nobody, neither journalists nor media moguls nor scholars, knows exactly where the mergers are taking us. The consequences of consolidation vary by media industry. And the evolution of communication technology is so fast that today's truisms can be undone tomorrow.

For now, anyone who wants to understand them will be best served by a healthy dose of skepticism, a search for illuminating facts and a willingness to consider *all* sides of the discussion. In that spirit, we offer the following caveats for journalists, media executives and the public from our contributors to this volume.

The best and the worst possibilities of the mergers have been articulated so loudly that everyone, especially reporters, should be on guard against both facile judgments and hyperbole. Despite the temptations to see the new communications conglomerates as monoliths, reporters should be alert to their internal differences.

Much of the merger story has fallen on the business and entertainment pages. While reporters there have done some good work, the transcendent economic, political and cultural importance of media consolidation also might be an argument for sustained treatment of this issue on Page 1. And reporters who cover the communications industry there should display the same kind of skepticism that they would bring to politics.

As conglomerates grow, journalists find themselves bundled up with entertainment divisions. Reporters need to be wary of challenges to their news values that can come from either corporate leadership that doesn't understand the need for newsroom autonomy or that confuses reporting and show business.

If the fusion of big news and big business is unavoidable, corporate parents need to learn as much as they can about journalistic ethics, the proper standards for their relationships to their news divisions and the need to serve the local, as well as the national, audience.

In an era when the role of government as a regulator of communication is dramatically revised, journalists can do more than they have done up to now to provide a forum for the fair discussion of the government's role in media regulation.

In all the rush to new media and big media, as journalists try to break through the clutter, certain elements of "old media" will remain valuable and perhaps more important than ever: good reporting, solid editing and good storytelling.

Today, when no one is sure what the future will bring, leaders in both the communications industries and news organizations need to "think outside the box"—to examine ways of working, managing and reporting the news to meet the new needs of new times.

Just as it is impossible to take in a grand vista with a single glance, so it is impossible to understand something as big as the mergers from only one perspective. *Media Mergers* approaches the emergence of media giants from a variety of angles. Our contributors offer many ways of understanding their scale and their significance. Together, they can help us come to more solid judgments about this brave new world of media.

Nancy J. Woodhull
Robert W. Snyder

I

Point/Counterpoint

1

Not So Fast

Todd Gitlin

The typical media report about media conglomeration is supercharged with the rhetoric of the conglomerates themselves. Fusing a business story with a celebrity story, it stresses the glamour of deal-making and the size, complexity and hypothetical synergy of the composite firm. Murdoch/ Disney/Time Warner/TCI is said to be sprawling through hardware and software, space and cable, wires and wireless, news and entertainment to bestride the earth. Stock analysts opine that the latest move of the week is somebody's coup. The burning question of the hour is, What's on the mind, the walls, the menu and the feet of Gerald Levin/Ted Turner/Rupert Murdoch/Michael Eisner/John Malone/ Sumner Redstone/Barry Diller as this colossus contemplates the deal of deals? The journalism of the awe-filled room is usually too busy to ask what these immense mergers and acquisitions mean for American—that is, world—culture. That's not the beat of the breathless chronicler. Nor are the prognosticators called to account for their previous financial projections, the ones that misfired.

Meanwhile, critics of the conglomeration juggernaut stress the danger of censorship. In television, there are a few reported cases, enough to worry about, though the argument as usually presented is not rigorous enough. NBC in particular seems to have gone lightly reporting allegations against the parent company, General Electric. According to the television reporter Marc Gunther in *American Journalism Review* (October 1995), a 1989 "Today" segment on defective

3

bolts failed to cite GE, which used said bolts for nuclear reactors; "Today" mentioned GE only in a damage-controlling follow-up. A 1990 "Today" segment on consumer boycotts, Gunther adds, omitted any mention of a campaign against GE itself, and one guest has said that a producer cautioned him not to bring up the GE case. (NBC said this was the producer's say-so.) But Gunther goes on to note that since 1990, NBC has covered GE scandals unobjectionably. It will come as no surprise if other such cases turn up nevertheless. Self-censorship, in any case, is probably the worse danger, but it is rarely expressed—it leaves no smoking memos.

But just how rip-roaringly fearless were the networks in the good old days when Paley, Sarnoff and other founding titans roamed the earth? The case against GE as such would be more impressive if critics compared NBC coverage of GE before its acquisition of RCA with coverage afterward. For that matter, does NBC cover GE differently than ABC, CBS and CNN do? Did it before, when NBC belonged to RCA, a major military contractor among other things, not exactly the corner grocery store? Did CBS cover nuclear power questions more assiduously before Westinghouse, a nuclear power, purchased the company? It's not clear. And one reason it isn't clear is that none of the television networks, regardless of who exactly holds title, lusts to expose the depredations of business. In the spirit of this political moment, television news at large has been far more ardent in pursuit of government red tape than in pursuit of industrial crime.

Conglomerates would seem to be set-ups for conflicts of interest between news and entertainment. *Time*, after all, as Gunther points out, devoted a cover story to Scott Turow, a Warner Books author, timed to the Warner Bros. release of the movie *Presumed Innocent*. *Time* found Turow more newsworthy than *Newsweek* did. *TV Guide* and the *New York Post*, both controlled by Murdoch's News Corp., have recently come under attack for showing favoritism toward programs on Fox, also owned by Murdoch. *TV Guide*, for instance, was criticized for a December 1995 cover featuring the low-rated Fox show "Party of Five"—"The Best Show You're Not Watching." On the other hand, *Time*'s coverage of the Bob Dole/William Bennett attack on gangsta rap did not fawn on the parent company and was no more—or less—superficial than *Newsweek*'s. Movies and celebrities are the stuff of cover stories whoever the owner is. In any event, to investigate the impact of mergers, it won't do simply to ask, say, Joel

FIGURE 1.1
Public Opinion on Mergers

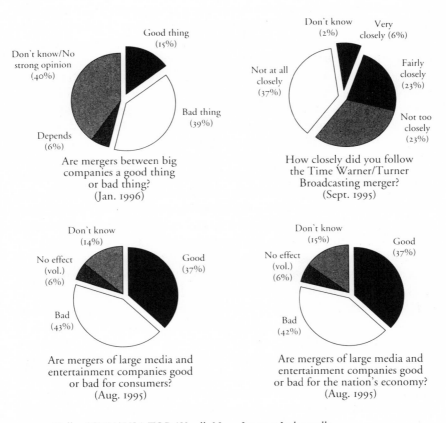

Are mergers between big
companies a good thing
or bad thing?
(Jan. 1996)

How closely did you follow
the Time Warner/Turner
Broadcasting merger?
(Sept. 1995)

Are mergers of large media and
entertainment companies good
or bad for consumers?
(Aug. 1995)

Are mergers of large media and
entertainment companies good
or bad for the nation's economy?
(Aug. 1995)

SOURCES: Gallup/CNN/*USA TODAY* poll; News Interest Index poll;
Princeton Survey Research Associates/*Newsweek* poll

Siegel of "Good Morning America" whether he plans to go light on
Disney releases. What would you expect a self-respecting reviewer to
say? Would any reviewer survive in any major publishing outlet today
who did not gush about a hefty share of Hollywood releases?

More worrying by far than petty backscratching (or backstabbing)
is the long-term chill—the sum, over months and years, of 1,000
microdecisions made by 1,000 personnel about 1,000 stories that it
seems, well, *injudicious* to push too far. Worrying is the closure of

news that comes from closure of bureaus and miscellaneous cost cutting. (The networks have precious few researchers as it is.) It stands to reason that reporters will also hesitate to take the risk of stepping on exposed toes. The larger and farther flung the enterprise, the more toes, and therefore the greater the risk for reporters. What was Cap Cities/ABC's Thomas Murphy signaling when he chided "Good Morning America's" Charlie Gibson for doubting how glorious it would be to work for the Disney "family"?

Already, in fact, the networks and papers alike have shown precious little interest in the momentous telecommunications legislation that Congress just passed in a snap and the president signed. The fragment of the bill that concerned the V-chip received more news attention than the rest of the bill put together—the increase of license periods to eight years, for example, and the easing of ownership restrictions. Now, single-ownership papers may or may not have been more likely to cover these questions than the chains have—this is pretty serious, complicated stuff for today's American newspapers. But aren't these questions worth contemplating at a leisurely pace before irreversible mergers are blithely waved through by a government afflicted by deregulation mania?

The case against the ill effects of conglomeration is strongest and best researched in the case of newspapers. The 12 largest chains control almost half of daily circulation. Chains, especially those that trade on the stock market, are more eager than single-paper proprietors to raise profit margins. They tend to cut costs by firing reporters and editors. As the number of newspapers in a chain goes up, the size of the newshole tends to shrink. Soft-news coverage goes up. Local coverage may increase or decrease as a percentage of the whole, but the articles tend to get shorter in either case. As for local TV, serious reporting is scarce enough there but is more likely to be found on the occasional independent station (like Oakland's KTVU) than from a station owned by a network or a chain.

Not nearly enough attention has been paid to the consequences of conglomeration in book publishing. At this writing, there remains one independently owned major commercial publishing company in New York (W.W. Norton). In general, the giants seem more reluctant to publish the so-called midlist. They are far less willing than before the great wave of mergers in the 1980s to use their cash cows to subsidize less commercial but worthy authors throughout what may turn out to be unremunerative careers. Like Hollywood studios, they bet big on blockbuster prospects. This does nothing for the culture but make fortunes.

The fate of publishing is also inextricably linked to the growing weight of chain bookstores. The *New York Times* reported, remarkably enough on its front page, the open secret that many people in publishing already knew: that Barnes & Noble, the nation's dominant chain, has been taking payments from publishers for premium space. A pile of books in the window, at the entrance or at the end of an aisle is not a sign that a bookseller has made a judgment of quality, nor even a measure of sales volume. It is a measure of subsidy. Even strapped independents are said to be resorting to this practice.

The point is not that the media were once fearless and are suddenly in danger of becoming fearful, or that entertainment was once stupendous and is suddenly in danger of dumbing down. (Network television in the fabled '60s, for instance, was largely brain-dead.) The point is that the changes now in progress are largely irreversible, potentially consequential, and they are being left to marketeers whose commitment to the public is dubious. The fact of diversification is being offered up as proof that there's no danger.

Now it is true that two phenomena have grown simultaneously in America's media. One is conglomeration. The other is segmentation. Demographic slices are the targets in cable TV, radio, magazines. If choice is the champion goal, then the more choice the better; and clearly Manhattan's Time Warner Cable, with 76 channels, cannot be worse for consumers than the precable array of seven VHF channels. Can it?

Not in the obvious sense, although the proprietors of cable TV have a lock on access. These effective monopolies permit and deny access just as they choose. Accountability is not their game. Giving preferences to their corporate partners is. So is catering to high-spending demographics. But even beyond cable, the standard of comparison ought not to be the impoverished past. The relevant question is about democratic potential. No one who worries about media trusts proposes a return to the narrow pipeline of yesteryear. The question is, What variety of diversity will the titans indulge? Most likely, immense varieties of segmented entertainment.

The thoughtful discussion of ideas is at a premium. The spiral of triviality winds onward. When the possible harms are great and potentially irreversible, is this not a matter for public inquiry? Surely Congress and the press might spare 10 percent of the time, money and energy they have devoted to petty scandals involving the onetime governor of a small state for the rather more momentous question of the impact of centralized power on the nation's sluggish flow of ideas.

The point is that the mergers are taking place amid a deafening silence. Trusts with the capacity for overbearing power are being merged and acquired into existence as if there were nothing at stake but stock values. Today's deals may weigh on the culture for decades. The potential for harm is at least as impressive as the potential for good. If the country believed in the countervailing authority of the government, the recourse would be obvious. It's time for the sheriff to step in and say, Not so fast. But the sheriff has been disarmed—at least politically. It suits the parties in power to collect impressive sums from the titans while proclaiming the virtues of self-regulation. If the issue were street crime, conservatives would be crying out against this abject surrender. They would be declaring that we must take the country back, city by city, newsstand by newsstand, frequency by frequency.

Todd Gitlin is professor of culture, journalism and sociology at New York University. His most recent book is The Twilight of Common Dreams: Why America Is Wracked by Culture Wars.

2

A Golden Age of Competition

Steven Rattner

It is truly ironic to be assessing the impact of mergers on media competition just as we are entering what may well prove to be the golden age of competition in communications industries.

Look in almost any direction and you see developments that will benefit consumers. In Washington, Congress has just enacted long overdue legislation that will rationalize an outmoded regulatory apparatus and free giant telecommunications and cable companies to battle each other. In New York, an array of news and financial services is being launched by equally giant media companies. Around the country—particularly on the West Coast—smaller, fast-growing companies are fighting to dominate the Internet.

Why is all of this happening now, particularly at a time of such high merger activity? The explanation begins with technological change. Just a couple of decades ago, most Americans had access to only a newspaper or two, some magazines and three or four television stations to provide their information and entertainment. No cable, with its 70–plus channels of programming, no VCRs or video stores, no satellite dishes, no computer on-line services and just a single provider of local and long-distance telephone service. In the television world, as recently as 1984, the three traditional networks—ABC, NBC and CBS—had 69 percent of the viewers (while cable had 14 percent).

The changes since then are familiar but dramatic. Cable now brings us debates about national policy—albeit at various levels of civility—

24 hours a day. For news and public affairs, we can now supplement the Big Three networks with Fox, two channels of CNN, C-Span, CNBC and, in many markets, one or more local all-news channels. As a result, by February 1996, the networks' share had dropped to 42 percent and cable's had grown to 27 percent. (For consumers to whom cable is not available, nearly a half-dozen satellite services—which were not around 10 years ago—now provide much of the same programming.)

That's not nearly the end of the story. The cable television companies are busily rewiring to provide not 70 channels or 500 channels or even 1,400 channels but, in effect, an infinite number of channels through video-on-demand. The result will be a vast array of new services, including shopping, games, information retrieval, transactions and much more.

Inevitably, these developments will take longer and cost more than many expect. But make no mistake about it, these services are coming. In just the past few months, we have witnessed proposals for a new Dow Jones/ITT financial news network (in addition to CNNfn, which has just been launched) and three news channels (ABC, msNBC and Fox).

All of these developments will give consumers of news and information more quantity and a greater degree of personal choice. For example, as Time Warner's test in Orlando has demonstrated, the cable companies have within reach the ability to provide consumers with the capacity to create their own news programs by instructing a "smart box" to select segments that are of particular interest.

It is difficult to overstate the importance of the Internet in providing a diversity of views. Its arrival brings with it the opportunity for any wannabe publisher to realize that ambition with as little equipment as a personal computer and modem. Thousands of 'zines have sprung up, of varying degrees of sophistication and insight, ranging up to the glossy entry promised by Microsoft when it hired Michael Kinsley of the *New Republic*.

Should you doubt the consequences of this technological change, consider the analogous development of the telephone industry. Only 12 years ago we had a single long-distance telephone company. Today, thanks to technology that allows consumers to change their long-distance carrier almost as easily as they order an item from a catalog, we have 17 major ones. And most significantly, since 1986, the price of long-distance telephone service has gone down 34 percent. (These lower long-distance prices have a further benefit in providing Americans with lower cost access to the Internet and on-line services.)

As for the front-page media mergers, they are certainly taking place. Many of the participants are large, powerful and familiar to all of us. The Disney/Capital Cities/ABC merger brought together two of the world's most respected companies. The Time Warner/Turner deal could create the largest entertainment company in the world. Westinghouse bought CBS, and the sale of MCA brought an important new corporate parent to Hollywood.

While these deals had the highest price tags and generated the most public interest, an equal level of activity has occurred off the front pages. In 1995, more than 160 television stations and more than 1,000 radio stations were sold, and ownership of cable television systems with millions of subscribers has changed hands.

All told in 1995, American media companies set new records in merger-and-acquisition activity, with announced deals reaching $93 billion, 85 percent higher than in 1989, the year many saw as the apex of merger-and-acquisition activity on Wall Street. Media deals have also been rising as a percent of total deals.

As technology continues to change and as we continue to update our regulatory apparatus to take account of these developments, further merger activity is certain to result. In this regard, it is important to appreciate that even after all of the aforementioned activity, the media industry in the United States is not particularly concentrated by any standard.

That is not to say that I do not share in the desire for competition. I do. But in defining competition, it is important to emphasize that size is not the principal issue, although by that standard, even the largest media companies are not among our biggest companies. The market capitalization of the new Disney, for example, will be around $54 billion, only enough to rank it the 15th largest American company. Time Warner's market capitalization after the acquisition of Turner will be around $36 billion. Compare that to Coca-Cola at $102 billion or Philip Morris at $98 billion, to take just two examples.

More relevant to the question of competition are measures such as market share and the barriers to a new company entering the same business. As I argued earlier, the huge increase in the number of cable networks indicates clearly the trend toward fragmenting market shares

FIGURE 2.1
Mergers and Acquisitions: Media Industries vs. All Industries

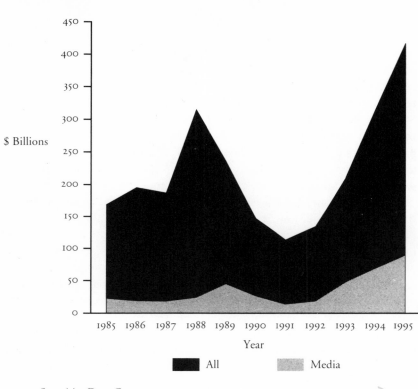

SOURCE: Securities Data Corp.

and lower barriers to entry in this sector, among others. These are true measures of competition.

In the cable television industry, Time Warner and TCI have emerged as giant operators, controlling a combined 40 percent of the market. But the 10th largest owner has over 1 million subscribers—an asset value in excess of $2 billion—and the 100th largest owner has 10,000 subscribers. In other words, there is still a long way to go before cable's level of consolidation approaches that of the telephone companies.

Nor do I despair that many of our journalistic enterprises are owned by large corporations. If anything, companies like Cap Cities have demonstrated that the result of corporate ownership can be freer and better journalism than we had when a few press lords controlled many of our newspapers and television networks. And the basic difference between the press lords of yesterday and the media moguls of today is that the press lords often ran their papers as vehicles for their own ideology and personal ambition. Today's moguls, with a few exceptions, seem more interested in making money than in seeing the triumph of their own ideology or personal ambition.

Another fear critics have of these mergers is that the ownership of journalistic organs by large corporations will inhibit the coverage by those journalists of their parent company. First, even if that were the case, so many other outlets would provide unvarnished reportage that the American people would hardly suffer a material loss. Secondly, many examples exist of tough reporting about a journalistic enterprise's parent company. For example, *Time* has published thorough, unbiased coverage of many Time Warner issues, from gangsta rap to the Turner acquisition.

Beyond not diminishing competition or quality, many of the media mergers have brought benefits. In some cases, they have provided the capital needed to launch exciting but expensive new undertakings. For example, the sales of cable companies have in many instances provided the financial resources to upgrade the systems so that all of the aforementioned new services could be provided.

In other cases, different skills have been brought together under a common roof, with the promise of exciting new offerings. Even though their deal hasn't closed, Time Warner and Turner have combined to produce a Time-CNN "AllPolitics" service on the Internet, offering more depth and more data than either entity can provide in its traditional format.

I agree that the nature of the media industry suggests a special need for attentiveness on everyone's part. Maintaining a diversity and plenitude of views—as well as freedom of expression—is critical to our democratic process. There may be a few instances, like the Newspaper Preservation Act, where a special role on the part of government is appropriate in order to maintain the greatest possible diversity of views. But these situations should be few and far between because the more that government views itself as having a special role with regard to the media, the greater the risk of government interference with the free expression of views. In general, the government should approach communications companies as it approaches other companies: with a clear role limited to applying our antitrust laws to ensure that a competitive environment is maintained.

Today, it is often suggested that American journalism has lost too much of its seriousness and too often has become trivialized. For the most part, that is a subject for a separate discussion, although I am convinced that to the extent journalism today is less thoughtful, mergers are not to blame. I am equally certain that, if anything, when the history of media in the latter part of the 20th century is written, it may well be concluded that we are in a golden age of information.

Steven Rattner is a managing director of Lazard Frères & Co. LLC., where he specializes in media mergers and acquisitions. He is a former New York Times *reporter.*

II

The Imperial Moment

3

What Does It All Mean?

Leo Bogart

The Telecommunications Act of 1996 has been hailed as the harbinger of a new era of expanded competition that will bring faster technical advances, greater consumer choice and more economical, efficient services. The Act signals a transformation in the media system and its economics. But, although it is intended to unbridle the free forces of the market, it may well end up accelerating the concentration of media power.

The process of concentration in the communications business is not unique; it has parallels in every other sphere of the American economy. Between 1985 and 1995, the share that the Fortune 500 leading corporations represent of gross national product rose from 44 percent to 63 percent. The economic forces that lead to mergers (shared distribution systems, use of complementary facilities and skills, and other economies of scale) apply as well to communications as to other industries.

The consequences for communications, however, are far more serious. Concentration in other industries may lead to market power, oligopolistic pricing and restrictive trade practices. In the media business, it can change the country's values, ideas and politics, perhaps even the national character.

The Telecommunications Act recognizes that individual communications, like phone calls and faxes, no longer exist in a separate universe from mass media. In the era of the Internet and the CD-ROM, of digitized and compressed information, the old boundary lines are mean-

17

ingless; no purpose is served by limiting a corporation's right to find wider applications for its skills and capital. Long-distance and local phone companies, cable and broadcasting systems are all allowed into one another's businesses.

The imminent prospect of the new legislation surely weighed in as a factor in the thinking of those who unveiled the great merger designs of 1995: Disney and Capital Cities/ABC, Turner and Time Warner, Westinghouse and CBS. Several provisions of the law must have been especially appealing—the lifting of controls over cable subscription rates, the opportunity for broadcasters to provide digital information services, the end of any restrictions on the number of radio stations a single company can own and the rise in the number of television stations it can own (to coverage of 35 percent of the population). Because of these changes, securities analysts agree that more mergers and acquisitions are in the offing, especially for smaller and middle-sized broadcasting and cable properties. US West is acquiring Continental Cablevision. Mergers of regional Bell operating companies (like those of Pacific Telesis and SBC, and Nynex and Bell Atlantic) will strengthen their ability to offer long-distance telephone service and give them the additional resources they need to become significant forces in providing video and electronic information.

Outright mergers are only the tip of the iceberg. An increasingly tangled web of alliances, partnerships and other connections embraces all the players in the global communications game. Companies engage in joint ventures that permit them to pool capital, spread risk, share information, acquire talent and expertise, and explore unfamiliar markets. Since communication is not in the least delimited by national boundaries, domestic competitors often find it expedient to collaborate when they start operations in a third country.

The cozy personal ties forged by corporate executives engaged in such common activities reinforce those already established at meetings where industry leaders mingle with their peers. In another period of history, business competitors may have kept a formal social distance from each other. Today they are thrown together to talk shop on innumerable intimate occasions. Collusion is osmotic and spontaneous; it requires no deliberate or sinister intent. In a system that must confront and master new technical marvels every day, media deals unravel almost as rapidly as they are made. Any catalogue of common ventures or investment positions is out of date as fast as it is compiled.

It is no longer possible to separate communications services from electronics manufacturing or from the preparation of computer software. Two notable cases are Matsushita's disastrous acquisition of MCA and Sony's thus-far unsuccessful foray into mass entertainment. Hughes Electronics, a division of General Motors, is the principal owner of the DirecTV satellite broadcasting system, in which AT&T has acquired a stake. MCI Communications will be investing as much as $2 billion in Rupert Murdoch's News Corp., though with a reduced stake in its Delphi service on the Internet. MCI is also in partnership with General Electric, through the NBC Supernet news service, and has jointly moved with Microsoft to exploit the World Wide Web. (Sun Microsystems, another software company, is also there.) Microsoft is a partner of DreamWorks SKG, the new producer of film and television movies. Tele-Communications Inc. (TCI), the nation's largest cable operator, owns a one-fifth share of the Microsoft Network, which was offered to Windows 95 buyers at half the price of other on-line services. TCI has a partnership with Sprint. Its one-fifth piece of Turner Broadcasting will make it the largest stockholder in Time Warner when the Turner merger takes effect. Meanwhile, News Corp. (which is working with TCI on a satellite TV sports channel and, along with US West, on another project on its BSkyB in the United Kingdom) is a partner of MCI in a satellite television venture. Dow Jones is a partner of General Electric's CNBC in European cable television and of TCI in Asia.

The situation is further complicated by the appearance of wild cards from outside the communications business: Seagram's Edgar Bronfman Jr., already a heavy investor in Time Warner, has acquired 80 percent of MCA; Kohlberg Kravis' K-III owns *New York* and *Seventeen* among its string of magazines; Revlon's Ronald Perelman is the main owner of New World Communications, a major television station group in which News Corp. also has a stake. This kind of interest in acquiring media properties is reminiscent of the eagerness with which 19th-century railroad and mining magnates bought newspapers. Then, as now, media ownership brought political influence that could be translated into monetary terms. Today, a big motivation seems to be ego satisfaction and entree into the celebrity realm of show business (of which news gathering has become an accepted component).

But money remains the real lure. As long as capital gains are taxed at a lower rate than dividends, a strong incentive for corporate consoli-

FIGURE 3.1

**Main Street and Wall Street: Volume of Consumer Spending on Media vs.
Volume of Media Industries Mergers and Acquisitions**

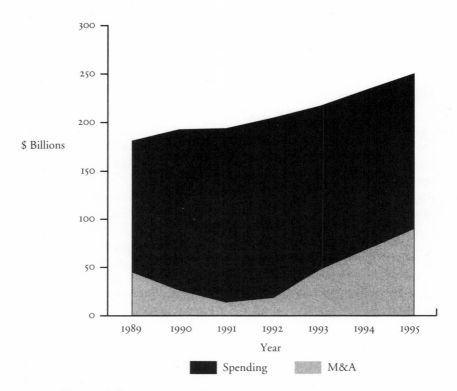

sources: Veronis, Sulher & Associates; Securities Data Corp.

dation is to drive up the price of the companies' stock, at least during
the takeover wars. This is generally good for management holders of
stock options, though not necessarily for stockholders in general. Share
prices often slide after such mergers, which usually dilute the existing
stock and saddle the merged company with the huge debt required to
finance the takeover. (After eight years, Time Warner stock has still
not recovered).

Yet the media companies do make a lot of money. In the 1980s and

'90s, their profitability has far outstripped that of American industry in general. It has been fueled by the public's apparently inexhaustible appetite for diversion, and by a willingness to give all forms of it—including gambling as well as mass media—a growing share of disposable income. As a result, the price of entertainment paid for directly by the public has shown considerable elasticity. (In the past 10 years, the prices of books, musical recordings and film admissions have risen roughly half again as much as the consumer price index. So has advertising cost per thousand.)

In the communications business, both horizontal and vertical integration appear to offer advantages. The distinctive boundaries between historically separate media have been obliterated by new technology. Common ownership makes possible a more diversified exploitation of successful new products, of information resources, of brand names and icons, of entertainment personalities, of new production techniques. It facilitates cross-media promotions, as well as instant and preferential access to distribution channels. The accepted wisdom on Wall Street is that the money is in the content, not in distribution, but of course the content is worthless without distribution. This is why, in 1993, a Federal Communications Commission ruling to permit the re-entry of the television networks into the program (and eventually, feature film) production business shook up the balance of power in the entertainment world and became a strong spur to fresh deal-making. (This merely accents the point that, because of its very nature, the media business is continually being shaped and reshaped by government actions.)

Many economists will testify that corporate mergers work in the best social interest—by attracting investments to those enterprises that show the greatest promise of efficiency and productivity. But media performance must be judged in social, political, moral and aesthetic terms as well as by its economic efficacy. The quarterly earnings statement, quite properly, is used by Wall Street as the touchstone of management's adequacy. But is profitability the only proper measure of a firm that deals in the facts that shape history and the fictions that represent a nation's collective dreams?

The larger the media organization, the more attenuated and impersonal the relationship between creators of content and managementís' exercising fiduciary responsibility on behalf of their stockholders. This estrangement is all the more likely in diversified organizations, whose managers must avoid emotional entanglements with any individual components of their far-flung empires. Media mergers result in larger and more heterogeneous companies; the next wave of media mergers will inevitably involve companies whose origins are in nonmedia (and sometimes even noncommunications) businesses. Thus the effect will be to move content ever closer to what either may be called the main line or the lowest common denominator.

In the world of mass communication, idiosyncrasy and deviation from the established mold are associated with high risk. In spite of the revived popularity of old notions under such new rubrics as "niche marketing" and "market segmentation," the bulk of advertising investments still go in pursuit of the mass audience. To win the audiences that advertisers want requires an adherence to time-tested formulas. The results are a leveling of taste and a resistance to experimentation.

Media organizations that began with vehicles intended to reach "everybody" (like newspapers and the on-air broadcasting networks) have diversified into channels that provide advertisers with narrowly targeted audiences. This specialization has differentiated the public's tastes more in terms of personality than by social class. Special interest magazines cover fashion, gun fantasies, homemaking, sex, woodworking and a variety of other subjects, but those with intellectual pretensions count their readers in the tens of thousands, not in the millions. Radio stations attract listeners of different levels of age and urbanity, but only a handful broadcast classical music or serious discussion. Cable channels present news, old movies, court proceedings, sports, cooking advice, cartoons and reruns of prime-time shows, but very little of their programming aims at more sophisticated interests than those reflected in run-of-the-mill network programs.

The studied use of violence and obscenity in the pursuit of audiences stems from the very market forces the Telecommunications Act aims to liberate. This happens just when public broadcasting and the National Endowments for the Arts and Humanities are under congressional attack—a disturbing coincidence.

Media mergers may affect not only the merit of mass communications but the vital political function embodied in their news-gathering and opinion-forming activities. By encouraging expanded participation in the mass media business, the legislators who adopted the Telecommunications Act no doubt expect that the public will have an ever larger array of information resources and greater access to fresh ideas.

Indeed, early in 1996 both General Electric's NBC and News Corp. announced plans to initiate 24–hour news services in competition with CNN. Subscribers to on-line services already can get up-to-the minute news and financial data from Dow Jones, Reuters, the *New York Times* and a number of other newspapers. Only a confirmed pessimist and skeptic would argue that the media mergers threaten to quench the torrent of news from myriad sources in which Americans can immerse themselves if they wish.

All diversified media corporations stress the importance of giving their news operations full professional autonomy and proclaim the need for independence of action and competition among their individual components. (At the same time, they all preach the virtues of "synergy" as the rationale for gathering those components together in the first place under the corporate umbrella.)

Yet the concentration of ownership and control over mass communications cannot be considered complacently. The ability of the news media to serve the public interest depends on the professional freedom with which journalists can probe, investigate and report events or developments that require open discussion. That freedom is inevitably affected by cynicism, by pressure, by compromise. When professional standards are questioned or disregarded in any news organization, other organizations take heed.

The processes by which this works are subtle and indirect. Few media overlords are so crude as to give direct orders to kill or slant stories. They do not have to do that in order to let it be known what their views are and where their interests lie. Almost imperceptible Pavlovian cues reinforce desired behavior and inhibit what is unwelcome.

In 1995, before the network's purchase by Westinghouse, CBS's "60 Minutes" dropped an interview with a disaffected executive of Brown and Williamson Tobacco who accused the company of manipulating nicotine levels in cigarettes in order to maximize their addictive effect. When the story came out, the network's defense was that it faced the serious threat of a lawsuit. CBS's then-principal owner, Laurence Tisch, was also the main stockholder of Lorillard, another tobacco company. The RJR Nabisco and Philip Morris companies, which own huge food and beverage businesses, are among the largest television advertisers. It is clearly impossible to determine what considerations entered the minds of the CBS executives who decided to kill the interview (which was ultimately broadcast, long after the episode had received widespread attention), or of the ABC executives who, in an earlier incident, apologized to Philip Morris rather than face a libel suit. However complex its motivations, self-censorship speaks for itself.

An important rationale for the media mergers is that they create giants with the financial and intellectual capital to compete effectively in the world's markets, especially those with the greatest potential to expand in the next century. Yet extraneous considerations multiply when companies' interests are extended, varied and substantial. And they are of special concern to companies that operate internationally and face the need to maintain the good will of intolerant and repressive governments.

At the news conference that announced the Disney Co.'s planned acquisition of Capital Cities/ABC, Disney Chairman Michael Eisner spoke enthusiastically about the opportunities in India and China. But the market he seemed to have in mind is essentially for time-filling apolitical pap. Foreign *entertainment* (in which sports is now a major component) is generally acceptable to the most repressive authoritarian regimes. *News* is not, as China has recently shown by its exertion of strict (and in the long run, unenforceable) controls over the Internet.

Yet, as Murdoch demonstrated when he withdrew the BBC World News from his STAR TV satellite broadcasts to China, the advertising revenues to be obtained from the satellite television market are too substantial to be risked by the demands of honest news reporting. Print media too are vulnerable. Among the world's news organizations, none value their integrity higher than the New York Times Co. and the Washington Post Co., the two principal owners of the *International Herald Tribune*. When a Singapore court imposed a heavy punitive fine on that paper for printing an article that correctly raised the issue of nepotism (in the appointment of Lee Kuan Yew's son, Lee Hsien Loong, to the deputy premiership), the *Herald Tribune*, inevitably with the knowledge and consent of its owners, decided to accept the judgment. There was a powerful pragmatic reason: It could not otherwise continue to print at that strategically crucial location.

The larger and more diversified the company, the greater and the more varied the corporate interests that may be threatened by crusading journalism. Consider Disney with its huge real estate and hotel holdings; Westinghouse, which, in spite of planned divestments, remains a huge manufacturing enterprise; or General Electric, with its long history of industrial pollution, its entrenched position in nuclear power and its intimate ties to the Defense establishment. (Apart from NBC, GE Capital is an important financier of radio and television stations.)

Under the new Telecommunications Act, the telephone companies, which have not heretofore been in the mass media business, will quickly emerge as major gatekeepers of content. Since their managements are instinctively averse to public controversy, they would tend to gravitate toward entertainment and away from news, accelerating a trend already under way. Amusement has acquired growing pre-eminence over information in the total time people spend with mass media.

Of much more serious and immediate import is the interdependence of communications firms and the various arms of government that determine the scope and terms of their activities. The very terms of the Telecommunications Act were arrived at by Congress under intense lobbying cross-pressures from local and long-distance phone companies, cable system operators and broadcasters. The same kinds of pressures have been applied in every previous legislative debate over media. They are felt by administration officials as well as by legislators, at the state and local levels as well as in Washington.

The pressures are backed by financial contributions from the political action committees that every industry has organized. In 1990 and 1991, at the behest of Ronald Crawford, a lobbyist for the National Cable Television Association, then Sen. Bob Packwood (a member of the Senate Commerce Committee) blocked bills to regulate cable rates. His diary revealed his reliance on campaign contributions from Crawford's clients: "The advantage Ron brings to me in the Washington PAC scene is that much of his income is dependent upon his relationship with me. He has got a vested interest in my staying in office."

The later-disgraced Sen. Packwood received $195,276 in contributions from telecommunications industry PACs between 1985 and the end of 1994. Altogether, that industry gave $39.5 million in political contributions during this 10–year period. A compilation by Common Cause found that in 1995, the seven regional Bell companies gave $941,590 in "soft money" (federally exempt) donations, two-thirds of it to Republican party committees. In the year's last week, when House Republicans declared the subsequently enacted bill "dead as Elvis," AT&T gave $200,000 to the Republican National Committee.

TABLE 3.1
Diverse Entertainment Operations & Assets of
Major Movie and TV Companies

	CableVision Systems	Disney	Gaylord Entertainment	General Electric	News Corp.	Seagram Co.	Sony Corp.	TCI	Time Warner	Tribune Co.	Turner Broadcasting	Viacom	Westinghouse Electric
New movies		•			•		•		•		•	•	
Film library		•			•	•	•		•		•	•	
Theatres						•	•		•			•	
TV shows		•		•	•	•	•		•	•		•	•
TV station(s)		•	•	•	•				•	•		•	•
Broadcast network		•		•	•								•
Basic cable network(s)	•	•	•	•	•	•		•	•		•	•	
Pay cable network(s)	•	•						•	•		•		
Cable or satellite system	•					•		•	•				
Recorded music		•				•	•		•				
Theme parks		•	•			•			•			•	
Pro sports	•	•							•	•			
Publishing		•			•	•			•	•		•	
Audio players							•						
Video players							•						
Retailing		•							•		•		

SOURCE: Standard & Poor's

When a powerful politician like House Speaker Newt Gingrich flirts on air with a powerful media tycoon like Tele-Communications Inc.'s John Malone, this reflects not just a common political philosophy but calculated material interests. The competition for cable channel allocations is acute, but Gingrich's new network, which bears the curiously Leninist name National Empowerment Television, got instant distribution in 7 million TCI households for its "Dateline Washington" program. At about the same time, Gingrich received an unprecedented $4.5 million book advance (later returned) from Murdoch's

HarperCollins. Coincidentally, Murdoch's Fox TV franchises were then under challenge.

The coming years will see a plethora of new deals and ventures on the part of communications companies. It is not very likely that communications empires with mass media properties will massage their news coverage to avoid offending the political powers that be. The real danger to journalistic integrity is not from the suppression of outrageous scandal but rather from the evasion of routine reports on the incompetence, stupidity and moral laxity of certain public officials whose interests and survival instincts happen to match those of corporate managements.

Would a *Kansas City Star*, given its new corporate affiliation with Mickey Mouse, be any less likely than under its former ownership to editorialize against the construction of a huge theme park next to a Virginia Civil War battlefield? Would it have taken a different position when owned by Capital Cities/ABC than in its earlier incarnation as an employee-owned daily? There is no way of answering such questions in specific cases, but they answer themselves as generalities.

Media mergers should arouse far less apprehension if control over content were separated from control over the channels of distribution, which properly should be common carriers. The communications giants would argue that the mechanisms of dissemination cannot be separated from the substance of what is transmitted, that what they sell to consumers is a package. But they are already making arrangements (as AT&T and MCI are doing to provide local telephone service) that pool their transmission facilities in the interest of efficiency. In fact they control not only what content is offered, but the ease of access to it (as governed by timing, channel position and the assembly of channels into pricing tiers). A cable system's decision to air the Comedy Channel rather than the History Channel is *not*—as is often argued— just another exercise of free speech. A franchise to broadcast or wire-up should be regarded as a public trust, not merely as a license to print money. That notion is not very prominent in the Telecommunications Act of 1996, nor in the executive suites of merged media companies.

Leo Bogart, a 1989–90 Media Studies Center senior fellow, is the former executive vice president and general manager of the Newspaper Advertising Bureau. His most recent book is Commercial Culture: The Media System and the Public Interest.

4

Fourteen Truisms for the Communications Revolution

Ken Auletta

Among leaders in the communications industry, insecurity is commonplace. Anyone with a modicum of sense is terrified by a business where technology means uncertainty, where consumer preferences are a mystery, where an ever more dominant Wall Street pursues its stock flavor of the month and where there is an insatiable media hunger for something new. It is of little surprise, then, that corporate chieftains pretend to know more than they do.

The captains of communication behave not unlike the apocryphal horse thief captured by the sultan. Sentenced to death, the thief pleaded for his life.

"Spare my life and I will teach your horses to fly!" he vowed.

The sultan was intrigued. So he granted the thief one year to perform his magic—or die. "How could you promise to make horses fly?" an incredulous friend privately berated the thief. "Maybe," the thief slyly smiled, "in a year the sultan will die. Maybe the horses will die. And, who knows, maybe the horses will fly!"

Any good CEO in the communications business has a bit of the horse thief in him. They pretend that horses can fly—and sometimes they do. Just 16 years ago, there was no CNN or MTV, no CDs, no faxes, no camcorders, no Walkmans—and, thankfully, no Madonna. Sixteen years ago people said the VCR would never fly. Today, a VCR is in nine out of 10 American homes. Five years ago, Rupert

Murdoch's News Corp. almost went bankrupt. Today Murdoch sets the pace in the race to become a global communications superpower.

Think about how quickly the paradigms change. A year ago, video-on-demand was the rage, but today the interactivity we speak of is the Internet. One moment, companies like Viacom complain that cable systems act like gatekeepers, denying distribution for their TV and movie products. The next moment, Viacom insists that software is king, and no distribution system can deny Viacom access. And now, once again, companies like Viacom fret that distributors like Murdoch can block access to entire continents.

It's a terrifying time to be involved in the $350 billion business of communications. We all wonder, Are there any certainties in the communications revolution?

Actually, there are some, and not all of them are comforting. They won't rival David Letterman's Top Ten List or Wilson's 14 Points, but in this era of communications confusion, there are at least 14 Truisms.

Truism 1: Companies Will Strive to Take the Risks Out of Capitalism

There is a method to the media madness we have come to call convergence. The blizzard of mergers and partnerships is motivated by good business reasons. The appropriate analogy for today's media business is 19th-century Europe. Instead of powerful nation-states we have seven potent industries: cable companies, Hollywood studios, broadcast networks, telephone companies, computer and consumer electronics, and publishing companies. Each industry, like each 19th-century nation-state, seeks to become a superpower. Beyond their pursuit of vertical integration, they use their power in one arena to increase their advantages in another. In other words, they seek leverage. Disney plans to use ESPN to assist its other cable networks. Murdoch's News Corp. erects direct broadcast satellite platforms all over the world, partly to gain influence over cable companies and other Hollywood studios. Leverage is why Microsoft bundled its new Internet connection (Windows 95) in with its popular computer software program (Windows). Every company wants to minimize the risk of capitalism by controlling every aspect of its business, from the creation of the idea to its manufacture and distribution to copyright ownership—and thus its afterlife. The bad news for consumers is that there will be too few global communication giants, and thus a risk of too few sources of information and entertainment. The good news is that technology is no friend of monopolies, making it possible for television, say, to be provided by broadcasters, cable companies, telephone companies, direct broadcast satellite, wireless transmission, computer—or even electric companies.

Truism 2: There Will Be More Competition—and Less

On the one hand, each industry prepares for war. The phone companies get ready to enter the cable business as cable plans to challenge the Baby Bells and broadcast stations. At the same time, every company hedges its bets by seeking the safety net of partners who share financial risks, provide absent skills or services and sometimes reduce political exposure. In the movie business, studios share costs—and profits—with producers. Think of some recent headlines: A long-distance company like MCI, which doesn't own software to distribute over its wires, invests $2 billion in a software company like News Corp. AT&T enters the video business by buying a stake in DirecTV, the nation's leading direct broadcast satellite service. Microsoft invests $500 million to help fund a 24–hour on-line news service with NBC. NYNEX pours $1 billion into Viacom. The same hedging notion motivates companies like Murdoch's News Corp. Fearful of protective overseas governments and nationalistic impulses, News Corp. has entered joint business ventures with the Chinese government.

For citizens, there are two vying future models. In one, the menace is that companies will agree to spheres of influence and say, "You stay out of my cable area, and I'll stay out of your telephone business. You stay out of England, and I'll stay out of Indonesia." Thus the promise of more competition contained in telecommunications reform legislation passed this year by Congress—that deregulation will result in more competition—may prove false. The alternate model, however, asserts that when government gets out of the way, unabashed capitalism is unleashed—with a consequent increase in competition.

Truism 3: There Are No Permanent Allies, Just Permanent Interests

And this is why an ally in one venture or country can be an adversary elsewhere. One week, MCI enters a joint Internet venture with

News Corp. Then it dumps this venture to join with Microsoft in a similar venture. The nation's largest cable operator, Tele-Communications Inc. (TCI), is an adversary of the US West in many states yet allied with US West in a joint venture in England. News Corp. and TCI are partners in creating both a worldwide cable sports network and a direct broadcast satellite delivery system in South America, yet they are currently adversaries in direct broadcasting in the United States. Universal and Paramount compete in the studio business yet jointly own the USA cable network, just as Hearst and Capital Cities/ABC compete in the magazine business yet are partners in ESPN. One needs a scorecard to keep track of these shifting partnerships.

Truism 4: The Playing Field Is Global

Communication companies no longer think of themselves as entities bound by national borders. As the U.S. market matures and other nations duplicate the deregulated environment pioneered here, U.S. companies often spy greater growth opportunities overseas. Today, roughly half of a studio's movie revenues flow from overseas. A company like Blockbuster explodes overseas. Ditto the U.S. music companies.

Truism 5: While the Playing Field Is Global, the Match Is Often Local

In this sense, Marshall McLuhan was wrong. We witness not the rise of a single global village, as he prophesied, but the rise of hundreds of local villages. American tourists in Europe or Asia may like to turn on their hotel TV sets and get the results of American baseball or football games, but a resident of New Delhi wants local soccer or cricket scores, local weather and local anchors. While McLuhan foresaw the way citizens of the world could watch the same event together—say, the Gulf War on CNN—he did not foresee how certain forms of technology—say, hand-held uplinks—would permit countries to create their own CNNs. At the same time, local playing fields impose constraints on global entrepreneurs. Murdoch believes in a free press, but not necessarily when it conflicts with his business interests in China (where he banned the BBC from his satellite service).

Truism 6: Brand-Name Recognition Is Everything

Familiar brand names are what can overcome the clutter of hundreds of channel choices. That's why NBC puts its brand on a global news service, a move News Corp. failed to make when it didn't put its Fox brand on Sky TV in Europe. The goal is to have a brand that instantly stamps a message on the consumer's brain—as MTV connotes youth, Disney child-friendliness and the *Wall Street Journal* business news.

Truism 7: The Distribution Business Is Not Dead Yet

In recent years it has been common to hear that software is king, that those who owned the cable wire could no longer act like toll collectors and decide which programming services got a channel on the cable box. It was said that as more wires competed to bring video to the home, distribution systems would become a commodity and lose leverage. Therefore, it was believed, a brand name like MTV would assure its own distribution. Today, lo and behold, studios want to own broadcast networks because the government now permits them to produce more TV programs. Each studio, then, wants to assure distribution of its television shows. Murdoch wants to start a 24-hour news service, but unless he has, say, a cable distribution system, he may not have one. Someday there may be 500 cable channels—or direct broadcast satellite may reach 100 million rather than 4 million homes—but until then, U.S. distribution remains a scarce commodity. And overseas, software factories like Viacom have learned that they need the permission of gatekeepers like Murdoch's satellite systems to reach viewers in Europe, Asia and South America.

Truism 8: Companies That Define Themselves Broadly Will Survive

The railroads atrophied because they thought they were in railroading rather than the broader transportation business. The networks declined partly because they defended their single channel and blindly fought the infant cable industry, failing to understand that they were in the entertainment and information business, not the single-channel business. Thus the danger for, say, the *New York Times*, would be to think of itself as being in newspapers as opposed to being in the information business. As long as customers pay to receive information from the *Times*, or advertisers pay the freight, it doesn't matter whether readers receive news on paper or off computer screens.

Truism 9: The Human Factor Matters

While covering Watergate, Bob Woodward and Carl Bernstein learned that they needed to follow the money to crack the cover-up. In covering the rash of mergers and firings in the communications business, however, we need follow more than business factors. We've got to follow the human factors—pride, greed, vanity, panic, personal comfort—behind the headlines. In an interview with me this January for the *New Yorker*, Time Warner CEO Gerald Levin spoke candidly of the uncertainty felt by business leaders in the rapidly changing communications realm. People are fired and deals are made, he said, on the basis of feelings as well as facts: "Many of these conflicts involve a CEO's comfort level. It's not always black-and-white when someone should be fired. It's judgmental. The most important thing is the feeling of a relationship. Words like *family* and *marriage* are important. In doing deals, you need trust, or they come apart. Wall Street often misses the point of throbbing emotionalism. Anytime someone makes a logical business decision, go look at the emotions underneath."

Levin fired first Robert Morgado and then Michael Fuchs as chiefs of Warner Music not because they were failures—by most business measures they were wildly successful—but because he felt uncomfortable with them. Similarly, Viacom Chairman Sumner Redstone fired CEO Frank Biondi because, depending on whom one believes, he either felt uncomfortable with his leadership or he envied Biondi's press clippings. Disney's Michael Eisner and Jeffrey Katzenberg divorced for human rather than business reasons. The proposed merger of Bell Atlantic and TCI collapsed as much for human reasons, like different corporate cultures, as for business reasons.

Truism 10: The Utility of the Information Superhighway Will Continue to Expand

Soon science will master the switched, digitized interactive network we have come to call video-on-demand and will make access to the

Internet a less fearsome process. The sophisticated set-top boxes will be ready, the complicated switching devices will be perfected, high-speed modems will be in place, and the video on computer screens will be as crisp as it is on TV screens. The era of 500–channel choices, or one channel that can summon any of thousands of programs, will be upon us. Children will be able to learn at home, to travel to distant places on their computer screens and ask questions. Schools will be able to wire classrooms to great teachers. Doctors will make electronic house calls, or instantly send X-rays to a specialist for a second opinion. We know the science we need to do all of these things, but . . .

Truism 11: No One Knows What Consumers Want

Do people want to program for themselves? Or do they prefer collapsing in front of their TV sets and letting network programmers decide what they will watch at 9 p.m.? Do consumers want to sit in front of television sets or computer screens? We know consumers want convenience (witness the spread of credit cards or bank-teller machines), but we do not know what video or computer services consumers will use. Will they accept the metered, pay-per-view universe favored by giant communication companies? Can they afford it? Will access to this video jukebox or the Internet be as simple as a remote control? Will there be enough customer demand to justify the huge investment companies must make?

Truism 12: The Communications Revolution Will Bring Profound Social and Political Consequences

Will we create two classes of citizens, the information haves and have-nots? What are the consequences of a society in which only 5 percent of low-income children have computers? What do we do, if anything, for the 90 percent of classrooms without access to a telephone, which is now the essential link to cyberspace? Who pays for it, the taxpayers or the communications companies? With unlimited communication and entertainment choices, will more Americans shutter themselves indoors and avoid face-to-face social interaction? Will the rise of virtual communities on the Internet decrease our tribal tendencies, or increase them and produce an electronic Bosnia? Will we read even less, as simple navigational devices like remote controls further attenuate attention spans? Will technology further heat up our politics by fostering instant opinions? New media will be more democratic, but will they allow the cool deliberation envisioned by James Madison and the Founders when they chose to divide power between the branches of government? We don't yet know whether Goliath companies will spawn monopolies or spur the growth of smaller, more nimble competitors. Will workers lose jobs, as 40,000 AT&T employees recently did? Will we benefit from more sources of news, or will giant companies with an eye on profit margins accelerate the trend towards infotainment?

Truism 13: The Marketplace Alone Will Not Determine the Outcome

Despite considerable talk about getting government out of the way, in many respects government will remain an 800–pound gorilla. In the United States, the federal government will decide whether to bring anti-trust action against Microsoft, whether to approve the merger of Time Warner and Turner Broadcasting, whether to lift restrictions on foreign ownership, and whether to allow broadcasters to inherit the extra spectrum space made possible by digital compression or require them to bid for it at auction. Will China continue to seek to regulate the Internet? Will France and Spain, among others, continue to erect barriers to foreign media competition? Will nations ignore copyright piracy? And will these actions trigger a trade war between governments?

It is tempting to think of the government gorilla as unthinking, but government has legitimate concerns—to protect privacy, to prevent monopolies, to promote the public good. Just as a football game would not be played without a referee, so government must often referee the contest between communication rivals. If the local and long-distance telephone companies, for example, are to compete and customers are truly to enjoy the lower prices brisk competition should bring, then government cannot be absent. For government must ensure that the local telephone companies or the long-distance companies rent their wire to competitors. Without a government referee, companies will have little incentive to cooperate. And if they don't cooperate, prices will not come down because AT&T, for instance, may have to spend enormous sums to lay its own local telephone wires, passing along the costs to customers.

Truism 14: It's OK to Be Confused

Many of us are nervous about how technology will alter our lives, and with good reason. And many of us are probably of two minds about the future. One part of my brain whispers: Remember how dire predictions have proved false. Television did not eliminate radio or movie theaters. The video store did not kill the studios. New media can arise without obliterating the old.

The other part of my brain whispers that things like video-on-demand and electronic news are fads, nothing more than this year's version of cabbage-patch dolls. It takes 43 minutes to scroll through 500 channels. Who wants to take a hand-held computer to bed in order to read when they could just as easily thumb through a book?

What is the realistic paradigm for the future—Cabbage Patch dolls or the life-transforming laptop? Will we be watching our TV or our computer screens? Will all the instruments of the home be merged into one? Which of the seven giant communication industries will war—or mate? Who will win, who will lose? Will government act as spectator or referee? What will consumers buy?

There can be no definitive answers to these questions because all of us are guessing. In the end, we rely more on instincts and feelings than hard facts. My own attitude is best summarized by Lewis Mumford, the noted urban historian, who once said: "I'm a pessimist about probabilities. And an optimist about possibilities." It is terrifying not to know the answers—and exhilarating.

Ken Auletta, a 1989–90 and 1994–95 Media Studies Center fellow, is the communications columnist for the New Yorker *and author of* Three Blind Mice: How the TV Networks Lost Their Way.

5

Media Regulation—New Rules
for New Times

Eli M. Noam

In an era of media mergers and cyberspace, any discussion of media structure should begin with this question: Are American media becoming more concentrated and controlled by a mere handful of companies capable of affecting politics and economics?

There are several reasons why the answer to this question is not an obvious "yes," despite the many recent media mergers. First, the media market as a whole, defined as the market for broadcast, cable, computers, software, print and content, has grown rapidly. While the fish in the pond may have grown in size, the pond grew, too.

To analyze the situation it is necessary to get some basic facts on concentration in the different industries that make up electronic media. Consider broadcasting. Concentration of ownership of radio stations nationwide is not substantial. In 1995, there were almost 12,000 U.S. radio stations. Yet the largest owning group, Jacor, owned only 54 stations. From 1987 to 1995, as regulatory ceilings were loosened, the percentage of the industry's revenue produced by stations owned by the top four group owners increased from 8.1 percent to 11.7 percent. In 1996, nationwide ownership limits for radio stations were eliminated altogether. This will likely lead to significantly larger radio station groups. Jacor, for example, has already bought or is about to buy 30 or more additional stations. But it would take vast purchases for the national market to become concentrated. On the other hand, since

39

local ceilings on radio station ownership were increased from one AM and one FM station per market before 1992 to up to eight stations in large markets today, instances of local concentration may occur.

In television, with the loosening of the limitations, concentration of ownership of TV stations nationwide increased from 1983 to 1995. The percentage of industry revenues earned by the top four owner groups grew from 15.2 percent to 22.2 percent. With the acquisition of CBS by Westinghouse, this will increase to about 25.8 percent. In most other industries, this share would not indicate a concentrated market.

Cable television shows significantly greater concentration. Locally, in 1992, only 1.5 percent of homes passed by cable had a choice of more than one cable operator. The top three cable firms serve 26 percent of cable subscribers and are vertically integrated into program supply.

The trend in programming sources shows great openness. Early radio was dominated by three networks: one owned by CBS and two by NBC. (The government forced NBC to divest one of these networks, which became ABC.) In 1938, 341 out of 660 radio stations were network affiliates. Today, commercial radio networks as a whole have been losing listeners, while the largest radio networks have grown slightly. The share of radio audiences held by the market leader, Westwood One (which had acquired NBC's radio network), increased from 6 percent in 1991 to 9 percent in 1995 as a result of acquisitions. This figure does not suggest market power. At the same time, the public radio network market also became more competitive, due to a government funding policy change in 1985 that enabled the emergence of competitive public radio networks such as Public Radio International.

In broadcast television, as a result of competition from cable networks and new Hollywood-affiliated broadcast networks (such as Fox, WB and UBN), the prime-time audience of the Big Three networks (ABC, CBS and NBC) dropped from 92 percent in 1976 to 53 percent in 1996.

In cable television, the diversity of programming has greatly expanded. In 1995 alone, 60 new channels were offered to cable networks, adding to the more than 50 channels that were already widely available. None of the cable networks individually attracts even 2 percent of the nationwide TV audience. Cumulatively from 1991 to

1995, the viewership of the top eight cable networks increased from 6.9 percent to a still-low 8.8 percent.

The telecommunications industry was distinguished for a century by AT&T's near monopoly until the 1970s when regulatory and technological forces combined to promote competitive entry. Even after the breakups, the various local exchange carriers a retained monopoly. Today, competitive access providers (CAPs) account for less than 1 percent, but their share has been increasing, especially among business customers, in those states that permit competition. The Telecommunications Act of 1996 oversees local competition in the remaining states. As a result, the local exchange market will likely be subject to more active competition by long-distance carriers, wireless providers, cable companies and resellers.

In long-distance telephone service, AT&T's market share fell considerably from 90 percent in 1984 to 55 percent in 1994. MCI and Sprint have about a quarter of the market; 500 other companies, mostly small resellers, account for 17 percent. The 1996 Telecommunications Act permits the Baby Bells to enter long distance, subject to opening of the local market. This, together with arbitrage by resale and new technological approaches such as "Internet phone service," is likely to drive prices further down and prevent oligopoly.

The contours of concentration in the computer field have shifted dramatically, too. Once, IBM dominated the U.S. computer industry; in 1969 it held more than 70 percent of market share. But technological developments, strategic mistakes at IBM and the shift from mainframes to PCs changed everything. In the critical microcomputer market, the top manufacturer in 1994 was Compaq with 12.8 percent. IBM's share was only 10.2 percent.

Concentration in the computer industry shifted to the operating system. Today, Microsoft operating systems are dominant. Partly due to its strength in operating software, Microsoft was able to reach market leadership positions in several important applications of software. This has fostered both a government antitrust lawsuit and an ongoing debate over the potential of competition through alternative technologies such as "network computers" that are independent of any particular operating system.

From a distance, the mergers and the increase in revenues generated by the major communication companies during the 1980s suggest an industry dominated by a few increasingly powerful firms. But a closer look at the corresponding market shares for the dominant communication companies of 15 years ago reveals that these companies are indeed bigger, but their control of their industry has declined. AT&T's revenues, despite its divestiture, increased from $40 billion in 1979 to more than $75 billion in 1994 (before its voluntary second divestiture that spun off equipment manufacturing and reduced the figure to $49 billion). Even so, AT&T's share of the information industry dropped from 24.4 percent to 11 percent (7 percent after the second divestiture). IBM revenues grew from $22.8 billion in 1979 to $64 billion in 1994, yet its share dropped from 13.6 percent to 9.4 percent. CBS, with revenues almost static at over $3 billion, saw its market share drop from 1.9 percent to 0.5 percent from 1979 to 1993. Only ABC, after mergers with Capital Cities and Disney, became part of a much larger media firm, accounting for 2.1 percent of communications instead of 0.2 percent in 1979.

What is the reason for these declines? The communication industry as a whole has exploded in the 1980s and '90s. And most of the growth occurred in the cable TV and microcomputer industries, which virtually invented themselves in this period. As new giants and small firms have emerged in these industries, the larger pie has been divided among more participants. In parallel, the advent of multichannel media has increased the diversity of delivery platforms and content available to users.

This is true for national concentration. But on the local media level, markets often remain concentrated because economies of scale exist that make entry difficult for additional telephone carriers, cable companies and newspapers. Thus, most homes have no choice in cable providers, and alternative local telephone providers have rarely served residential customers. Competition in multichannel video delivery and in local telephony is beginning to emerge only now. The Telecommunications Act of 1996 makes competition between cable and telephone companies likely: They will begin to compete in one another's markets in many local areas, substituting the economies of scope of multiple products for economies of scale. In addition, wireless delivery services for voice and multichannel video are offering increasing competition in these markets. Electronic delivery will also compete as an advertising vehicle with local newspapers, but that will only raise entry barriers to other newspapers.

What are the implications of these numbers? Electronic media industries in the United States have been evolving through three stages: in the past, the stage of *limited* media; now, *multichannel* media; and in the future, *cyber*media. Today we are constructing a new media system that is fundamentally different from its predecessors. Any regulatory system is therefore likely to be quite different from previous ones. The lengthy stage of limited media was defined by monopoly or oligopoly. Federal and state governments therefore set forth regulations to contain the market power of the few players: limits on broadcast station ownership, cross-ownership restrictions, rate regulation and limits on phone company activities. (These restrictions also often had the goal of protecting the exclusivity of those firms.)

Today's much more open multichannel media system dates, ironically, to about the year 1984, when media broke free from restriction on several fronts: Cable TV was deregulated, the telecommunications monopolist AT&T was split up, and the government had just dropped its antitrust suit against IBM due to the firm's loss of domination. In the multichannel phase, many of these restrictions were changed or lifted, as exemplified in the fundamental and sprawling Telecommunications Act of 1996.

Yet there is concern that regulatory liberalization has not led to openness and competition but to a new level of media concentration. And indeed, recent years have witnessed the expansion of large media firms in the United States through mergers, acquisitions and expansion. As a result, a small group of very large media firms—like AT&T and IBM—has emerged with revenues up to the $65–$80 billion range. (Although in comparison, General Motors, the largest U.S. firm, is two to three times as large.)

In the cybermedia stage, the lines between transmission systems blur as telephone communications, mass media transmissions and computer data exchanges are combined over an integrated, interconnected system of multiple digital broadband networks linked to video servers. In this context, continued use of a regulatory system that places different functions in a discrete regulatory box, and highlights the distinctions between them with cross-ownership prohibitions and other differentiated treatment, would be unworkable. It will also be largely unnecessary.

In the stage of limited media, regulation was justified by the principle of scarcity. When electronic media were so limited that only a few could gain access, regulation was required to ensure that those few served the needs of society without accruing undue benefit from their privileged position. In the stage of multichannel media, regulation was to prevent those with control over the gateways to the multichannel delivery systems from excluding competing providers from subscribers' homes.

In the cybermedia future, scarcity and gatekeepers will be largely eliminated. The future will not be one of 5,000 channels. Rather, it might well be, in the extreme, a future of *one* channel, an individualized channel for each individual, composed of various content components, assembled by personal electronic agents seeking a favored constellation of programs from a large menu of supply and delivery options. And there will no longer be an economic rationale for synchronous mass-audience channels once cybermedia enables advertising to be decoupled from content and targeted to specific viewers or classes of viewers regardless of what they view at that moment.

In such an environment, it is unlikely that sprawling media conglomerates combining all aspects of media will be successful. Vertical integration loses its power and becomes a drag. Different divisions of the same company would have competing objectives. To act with optimal efficiency in an open, competitive environment, each segment of a company must be willing to buy, sell or joint-venture with companies that compete with its parent company, if the rival offers better terms. Without market power in one market to leverage into another, extensive vertical integration rarely makes economic sense.

While there is much hype about the synergies created by vertical mergers, without market power at some stage of production, these benefits tend to be illusory. Hence, competitiveness in all segments of the communications industry is likely to reduce the economic logic for vertical integration and lead to more focused firms. Some companies are likely to restrategize and follow a "systems integration" approach, in which they do not own or operate the various activities of production and transmission but rather select optimal elements in terms of price and performance, package them together, manage the bundle and offer it to the customer on a one-stop basis. This will not require an actual physical presence in each stage or region; consequently, entry barriers will be lower.

The primary rationale for regulation has been the need to compensate for the imbalance of power between huge monopoly suppliers and small and technically ignorant users. In a converged environment with full choice, however, the imbalance will change. This will largely resolve traditional problems of price, quality, security, privacy and content diversity.

For some time, however, there will still be a need for regulation to create or ensure interconnection among networks and to maintain support mechanisms for universal connectivity. Since the media of the future will be more essential than ever to society—not just for entertainment, but for information, education, social services, work and participation in society and the economy—the value to society of having all its members connected will be more important than ever. Given the reality of politics, government is not likely to disappear from this area.

It is naive to argue, as many Internet enthusiasts do, that any regulation becomes "impossible." True, determined users can undercut any restriction. But as Internet applications create platforms for vast economic transaction, society will extend the scope of its controls, however wise or misguided they are, to the electronic medium and to the major players serving or using that medium. The notion that one cannot control the Internet is therefore ultimately deeply pessimistic, because it is a message of technological determinism in which society is seen as helpless. This is incorrect empirically and objectionable politically. We should choose liberty because we want to, not because we have to.

The United States has invested, at great political cost and effort, in a diverse communications structure. Today, the result is a dynamic market with considerable technological, artistic and business entrepreneurialism. Users have more choices and more tools for production, and the newest media system, the Internet, is a marvel of decentralization, democratic spirit and innovation. In that environment, traditional market structures are being eroded and recast. Major firms are vigorously trying to extend their activities vertically and horizontally. But as they grow, they also overlap and compete. There is no evidence of dominance comparable to the old triumvirate of AT&T, IBM and ABC/CBS/NBC. And should some dominance continue or be newly established, and not be contained by competitive market forces, reregulation will no doubt return by popular demand.

Eli M. Noam, a 1994–95 Media Studies Center fellow, is director of the Institute for Tele-Information and professor of finance and economics at Columbia University's Graduate School of Business.

III

Captains of Communication

6

Moguls Past and Present

Madeline Rogers

The only media mogul I ever encountered personally was the infamous Robert Maxwell. I was at the end of a 14–year career as an editor at the New York *Daily News,* which had been experiencing yet another stomach-churning dip in a years-long roller-coaster ride of shrinking circulation, strikes, buyouts, revolving-door management and serial flirtations with aspiring owners. It was October 1991 and the ailing tabloid (as it might have characterized itself) was in the fifth month of a strike. Desperately seeking a buyer, the owners, the Tribune Co. of Chicago, threatened to shutter the 72–year old daily unless the unions agreed to concessions. As the deadline approached and the unions stood firm, the owners accepted Maxwell's offer of salvation.

On the day of my brush with moguldom, Maxwell and his entourage sailed through the newsroom to greet employees. The British titan was straight from central casting: rotund, florid, dressed in Savile Row accessorized by Ringling (polka dots meeting stripes as I recall). Unfortunately, as we soon learned, Maxwell didn't just look too good to be true—he was. When he took a fatal plunge from his yacht just eight months after acquiring the *News,* many of his employees, creditors and pensioners here and abroad took a plunge with him.

Maxwell was a scoundrel but we wanted to like him, not only because he represented hope for the *News,* but because he appeared to have come out of the tradition of the *News'* founder, Joseph Medill

Patterson, an old-school titan whose personality was stamped onto every page of his newspaper. And editorial employees like to feel they are working for something that is more than a business, something that is a cause.

Now, Maxwell and Patterson are both gone. In today's media universe, dominated by impersonal corporate conglomerates, only Rupert Murdoch still seems to employ a management style that characterized the first media moguls, a seemingly contradictory blend of political beliefs, love of power and an instinctive bond with mass audiences. The earlier generation of moguls built empires on both passion and profits. In today's generation, however, the passion is fading.

Maxwell's criminal dealings ultimately distorted his life, but in his journey from poverty-stricken boyhood to the pinnacles of a global communications empire he walked a path followed by other tycoons. Like Maxwell, a number of moguls' life stories could have been penned by Horatio Alger. Allen Neuharth, founder of *USA Today*, brags of his rise "[f]rom a dollar-a-week butcher boy in South Dakota to a corporate CEO with annual pay of $1.5 million-plus." Frank Gannett's fortune began with a "drudging" boyhood that included a stint in a fertilizer factory. Joseph Medill, *pater familias* of the Medill/McCormick/Patterson clan of *Chicago Tribune* and New York *Daily News* fame, missed out on an advanced education when his family's farm was destroyed by fire.

Silver-spoon moguls who never had to deliver papers or shovel fertilizer often seem to have been downright envious of those who did. Joseph Pulitzer chose to leave the upholstered comfort of his affluent Budapest home and at age 16 volunteered to serve as a Union soldier in the American Civil War. William Randolph Hearst, who inherited his first newspaper, the San Franciso *Examiner*, from his wealthy father, never knew want. Nevertheless, he enjoyed casting himself as a renegade. Here is Hearst on Hearst in one of his peppery columns:

> Your columnist once knew a little boy named Willie.
> His mother wanted him to grow up and be a gentleman.
> Willie did not want to be a gentleman. He wanted to be a pirate . . .
> Willie never realized his ambition to be a pirate, but he got to be a newspaperman, which is in the same general category.

Hearst, like today's newest media giant, Bill Gates of Microsoft, attained admission to Harvard, only to drop out. Rupert Murdoch, the son of Australian newspaper magnate Sir Keith Murdoch, scraped through Oxford, where he was best remembered for his socialist views and the bust of Lenin he kept on the mantelpiece.

Economic status notwithstanding, many media moguls have felt a sense of exclusion that leads them to throw in their lot with the common man: Pultizer and Maxwell felt the sting of anti-Semitism; Patterson was cruelly taunted at Groton for his Midwestern accent; the Aussie Rupert Murdoch felt excluded by the British upper crust (and got his revenge by purchasing the revered *Times* of London in 1981). As outsiders by birth or inclination, media moguls have shared an appreciation for the masses or, perhaps more accurately, an appreciation for a lucrative mass market and a genius for reaching it.

Media moguldom was born in the three decades following the Civil War. The first newspaper barons and their empires came of age with the railroad, the telegraph and the modern corporation. In an astonishingly fertile period from 1880 to 1889, more than 625 newspapers emerged nationwide, the largest 10–year increase in the history of the press. The first great newspaper chain was founded by the Scripps family in 1873. Built on the success of the *Detroit Evening News*, the family holdings burgeoned into 24 dailies by 1937. This was the era of Pulitzer, who purchased the staid New York *World* in 1883 from the discredited railroad baron Jay Gould and built its circulation from 15,000 in 1883 to 250,000 in 1886. Hearst entered the fray in 1895 by purchasing the New York *Morning Journal*, igniting one of the most renowned and spirited circulation wars in the nation's history. By 1935, *Fortune* magazine valued Hearst's holdings—newspapers, magazines, radio stations, motion-picture companies, real estate, and gold and other mining operations—at $220 million.

It was a bloody period of mergers and acquisitions as wrenching and fast paced as anything we're witnessing today. Hearst was notorious for moving into cities, purchasing existing papers and then shutting them down or folding them into his empire. Mergers and chains made business sense: The owner of one newspaper had to supply it with newsprint, ink, staff and stories. The same owner with 20 papers could centralize his accounting functions, his sources of supply and his news gathering. The *Chicago Tribune*, for example, under the leadership of Medill's grandson, Robert McCormick, established its own Canadian paper mills. Hearst and McCormick both supplied their dailies with stories gathered by their own news syndicates.

The rise of newspaper chains, like the rise of other huge mass-production industries in the same period, grew from a blending of technology (the telegraph, the telephone, the rotary press, the half-tone process), new transportation networks, population growth and aggressive promotion. Of equal, if not primary, importance was the development of a bold editorial style that attracted a mass audience to newspapers in unprecedented numbers.

With few exceptions (Adolph Ochs and his *New York Times*, Frank Gannett and his staid small-city papers come to mind) the greatest media empires were built, and are still built, on an editorial product designed to entertain, shock, inflame and—occasionally—educate. Pulitzer signaled this new era in journalistic practice when he told the staff of his newly acquired New York *World*: "Heretofore you have all been living in the parlour and taking baths every day. Now I wish you to understand that, in future, you are all walking down the Bowery." Then, as now, new ownership prompted disgruntled editors and writers to hit the pavement in search of new employment.

Theories of how best to appeal to the unlettered or semilettered masses led to techniques that anticipated sound-bite journalism. Medill, as publisher of the *Chicago Tribune* for example, was an advocate of simplified spelling: He outraged his literate readers with spellings such as *infinit, favorit* and *telegrafed.* Hearst wrote in pithy paragraphs, often only one sentence long.

Not surprisingly, the mass press was reviled by the "classes." The writer Stephen Crane said of Hearst's brand of journalism: "I see no difference between the [New York] *Journal* and Hammerstein's roof garden. You get the blonde with the tin can in her gullet and the comic speaker and the song about mother's wayward boy in both shows."

As Crane implied, Hearst and his contemporaries presided over an unprecedented marriage of entertainment and news. It is a coupling that is accelerating today, but the motives have changed. Most of today's entertainment/news conglomerations—ABC/Disney, Fox/Murdoch, the proposed Time Warner/Turner merger—are driven purely by the bottom line. The men who lead them are thoroughly at home talking of business deals, but in general they cannot rally the public with a compelling vision. In contrast, the first generation of media moguls—the newspaper barons—sought profits but used their publications to further a political agenda, which in many cases grew out of the 19th-century reformist tradition.

The early titans' sympathy for the common people was fueled not only by a desire for circulation and profits, but by a hatred of the excesses of the Gilded Age, which they felt were inimical to the republic. Pulitzer created his own 10 commandments for his New York *World*, which included a promise to "always oppose privileged classes and public plunderers." Hearst was a self-declared enemy of "reactionary interests and predatory corporations"; Patterson, who dedicated his New York *Daily News* to Abraham Lincoln's "common man," was a socialist in his youth. In an article published in 1906, he reflected on the inequities of a society in which "[t]he work of the working people produces the wealth, which by some hocus-pocus arrangement, is transferred to me, leaving them bare."

The early media moguls were idea merchants who knew that technological innovations—paper, ink and presses—were the means of *reaching* readers but that editorial content was the key to *attracting* and *keeping* readers. Some of the early creators of television, dazzled as they were by the power of their new technology, also maintained a commitment to compelling content.

Today, the vast reach of media conglomerates—via television, radio and, most recently, the Internet—is something earlier moguls could only dream of. But it appears that as delivery systems become more sophisticated, the content suffers.

When Bill Gates predicts, in his 1995 bestseller, *The Road Ahead*, that our newest delivery systems will be useful for checking on rush-hour traffic, retrieving halibut recipes or selling a used Mustang, one wonders if technology hasn't leaped ahead of our current moguls' capacity to fill their media with meaning. Stay tuned.

Madeline Rogers, a former assistant managing editor at the New York Daily News, *is currently director of publications at the South Street Seaport Museum and editor of* Seaport, *"New York's History Magazine."*

7

Two Faces of Mickey Mouse

Loren Ghiglione

In the beginning, B.C. (Before Conglomeratization), a 1937 minia-
ture comic book featured Mickey Mouse writing and running his own
newspaper, the *Daily War-Drum*. Mickey exposed bribe-taking town
councilors and Looey the Leg's gang of racketeers.

Today Mickey Mouse symbolizes not the heroic editor/owner—the
independent journalist—but an ominous multinational, multimedia conglomerate, Walt Disney Co., which busily devours Capital Cities/ABC
and threatens independent journalism. A Mike Luckovich cartoon shows
cigar-smoking Mickey, owner of ABC television, ordering around news-
caster Ted Koppel. In a Paul Szep cartoon, ABC anchor Peter Jennings
gives way to Mickey reading mindless "mickey mouse" infotainment
fluff.

Those contrasting images of Mickey Mouse, the old symbol of
independent journalism vs. the new symbol of anti-independent, anti-
journalism megaconglomerate boob-tubism, summarize the two sides
of popular depictions of the American news business. Whether as
movie hero or anti-hero, the anything-to-get-the-story reporter has stood
for American journalism's freedom and power, its independence and
individuality. But the reporter's boss, the news media owner, has represented a more paradoxical, less appealing icon.

The owner has embodied not only freedom of the press, but also
freedom to oppress. In this vision, owners not only scoop competitors
but also destroy them. Orson Welles described Charles Foster Kane,

55

his movie version of William Randolph Hearst, as "at once an idealist and a swindler, a very great man and a mediocre individual."

Initially, the owner/journalist/printer was a pillar of the Republic. "The Country Printer," Philip Freneau's 1791 poem, portrays him as a defender of press freedom's "sacred cause" and as community-minded self-censor who emphasizes people's good qualities and conceals ill "from vulgar sight!" But in the early 19th century, in the age of partisan journalism, Charles Dickens, James Fenimore Cooper and other fiction writers took a harder look at the owner/editors of the partisan press. Those editor/owners abandoned principles, Alexis de Tocqueville wrote, "to assail the characters of individuals, to track them into private life and disclose all their weaknesses and vices."

By the late 19th century, as mammoth metropolitan newspapers came of age, ownership moved from the editor in the newsroom to the publisher in the counting room. Novels caricatured owners as stern, sinister snakes—right down to their names. In Henry Francis Kennan's *The Money Makers* (1885), Aaron Grimstone, a corrupt capitalist, silences an honest editor by buying his paper and firing him. Harriet Beecher Stowe's *My Wife and I* (1871) features Mr. Goldstick, a publisher who measures everything by its dollar value. In William Dean Howells' *A Modern Instance* (1882) and *The Quality of Mercy* (1892), Mr. Witherby, "the countingroom incarnate," owns "a journal without principles and without convictions, but with interests only."

In the early 20th century, these novels' depictions of media tycoons reverberated in silent films. In *The Little Wanderer* (1920), the crooked publisher exploits the poor to build sales. The publisher in *On the Jump* (1918), who spiked a story about Liberty Loans, turns out to be a German spy. Later, the talkies, reacting to the yellow journalism of the new circulation-hungry tabloids, continued the trend. Among Hollywood's vulgar vipers, ruthlessly pursuing money or power, were Berton Churchill in *Scandal for Sale* (1932), Otto Kruger in *Scandal Sheet* (1939) and Oscar Apfel as publisher Bernard Hinchcliffe in *Five Star Final* (1931).

The star of *Five Star Final*, Edward G. Robinson, plays Arnold Randall, an idealistic managing editor who bows to publisher Hinchcliffe's demand for sensationalism. Randall exploits a story about an ancient case in which a woman, now quietly married, killed an errant lover. The coverage leads to the "lovenest killings" of the woman, her daughter and the well-to-do man the daughter is about to marry.

Randall has already taken to washing his hands obsessively (imitating the real Emile Gauvreau, editor of the sensationalistic New York *Evening Graphic*, nicknamed the Pornographic) when he receives the telephone tip about the "lovenest killings" caused by his paper. He angrily erupts at the caller: "Hinchcliffe's got to get himself a new head butcher. I've had 10 years of filth and blood. I'm splashed with it, drenched with it. I've had all I can stand." Randall finally screams into the telephone, "Take your lovenest killings and Hinchcliffe with my compliments and tell him to shove it up his _ _ _." Randall throws his phone through the glass door to his office, and the shattering of the glass covers the sound of his shouted "ass."

Portrayals of newspapers in motion pictures of the 1930s weren't all seriousness. Part of the high spirits of *The Front Page* (1931) involved reminding the movie viewer that, in an owner's eyes, the newspaper was about business, but that in any self-respecting reporter's eyes, the newspaper was never about business or the owner. The newspaper owner, never shown in *The Front Page* and irrelevant to the movie's reporters, could be assumed to have the features of "the perfect newspaper owner" pictured in a cartoon that adorns a Poynter Institute classroom wall: "NO BRAINS—He owns a newspaper, right?" One of *The Front Page* reporters, Murphy of "The Journal," says, "I got a dumb brother went in for business. . . . He gets worse every year. Just a fat-heat."

The newspaper movies of the '30s, as film critic Philip French has written, culminated in *Citizen Kane* (1941), "a sort of combination of the high spirits of *The Front Page* and the liberal censoriousness of *Five Star Final*."

Liberal censoriousness permeates the love-hate portrait of Kane, the media mogul. In one sequence Jed Leland (Joseph Cotton), Kane's honest alter ego, reviews the "hopelessly incompetent" operatic debut of Kane's second wife. In his drunken stupor, however, he cannot complete the review. Kane finishes it without softening the criticism. He makes sure the review sees print. Then he fires Leland.

Hearst, of course, was just as imperious as Kane. When Hearst learned that RKO would portray him in *Citizen Kane* as a controlling conniver, he connived to control the movie. A Hearst flunky offered RKO's president $842,000, the movie's production and postproduction costs, if he would destroy the negative and all prints. RKO's president turned down Hearst. Then Hearst insisted his papers not review *Citi-*

zen Kane and other RKO movies. RKO stood firm. Hearst's power intimidated theater owners, and at first RKO could not find theaters— except its own—that would book *Citizen Kane.*

Over the past 50 years, Hollywood's media owner—an individual-istic, even idiosyncratic voice—has given way to the impersonal, profit-crazed, megaconglomerate boss. The action has shifted, writes histo-rian William McKeen, "from the newsroom to the board room." A newspaper company's founder or his widow falls prey to shareholders (often the owner's children), public stockholders or a spineless board of directors. The owner's company ceases as often as it survives.

Television dramas, novels and other forms of fiction treat the spread of newspaper chains and other big businesses as an attack on America; they romanticize the independent owner. In "Takeover," a 1977 epi-sode of the "Lou Grant" television series, Margaret Pynchon (Nancy Marchand), publisher of the "Los Angeles Tribune," owns 49 percent of the newspaper's stock. Her nephews control 49 percent, and the paper's attorney 2 percent. The nephews and the attorney agree to back a takeover bid by smooth-talking media tycoon Russell Grainger (John Anderson). But Grant (Ed Asner) and Pynchon passionately plead to maintain the "Tribune's" independence. "My God," says Pynchon, "we're not talking about a side of beef." Persuaded, the attorney votes in her favor. The takeover attempt fails.

Novelists also humble—and humiliate—avaricious media owners. In Richard Powell's *Daily and Sunday* (1964), the employee-owned "Mail" repulses the Knudsen chain ("its individual papers were too much alike, as if they were boxes of assorted cookies distributed under a national brand"). In Arthur Miller's *Final Edition* (1981), media czar Samuel Bradbury ("milk the last penny out of every property") fails to take over J.P. Hargrove's "Bay City Times." Some novelists reward the moguls with more than defeat. In Richard North Patterson's *Pri-vate Screening* (1985) an insane terrorist pushes newspaper magnate Colby Parnell to kill himself on national television. In Colin Watson's *Coffin Scarcely Used* (1981), publisher Marcus Gwill winds up elec-trocuted, his mouth crammed with marshmallows.

Death—of the newspaper, if not the owner—dominates post-World War II films about press potentates. In *The Fountainhead* (1949), Gail Wynand (Raymond Massey), the powerful owner of the "New York Banner," is proud to have escaped Hell's Kitchen. "I own most of it now," he says. "I rose out of the gutter by creating the 'Banner.'"

Wynand decides to save Howard Roark (Gary Cooper), a highly original (and stereotypically independent) architect who is under attack by the public and the rest of the city's newspapers. "I've never lost a battle," Wynand says. But the "Banner's" advertisers flee. The paper's board of directors insists that Wynand reverse his position. He does, cowardly siding with Roark's enemies. Roark miraculously survives, building the world's tallest building, the Wynand building. But the "Banner" dies. Wynand pulls a pistol from his desk drawer and kills himself.

In *Deadline USA* (1952), Margaret Garrison (Ethel Barrymore), widow of legendary owner John Garrison, fends off her majority stockholder daughters, Katherine and Alice, when they plan to sell "The Day" to competitor Lawrence White, owner of the substandard "Standard." Though he would net $50,000, Managing Editor Ed Hutcheson (Humphrey Bogart) opposes the sale to White. "He's eliminating his competition, that's all," Hutcheson shouts at the daughters. "You're not selling 'The Day,' you're killing it." "The Day" dies a glorious death: Its final edition carries a mob-defying front-page exposé. And the movie ends with the presses rolling to the tune of "The Battle Hymn of the Republic," which reminds us that "truth is marching on." But the "Day's" 290,000 subscribers no longer have their newspaper.

In *While the City Sleeps* (1956), Amos Kyne (Robert Warwick) runs nine newspapers, including the "New York Sentinel," and photo and news services. He qualifies as an old-fashioned, right-thinking owner who espouses "the responsibility of the free press to the people." So, of course, he dies only a few minutes into the movie, leaving the company to his spoiled, playboy son, Walter (Vincent Price). Walter pits three managers against one another and promises that the one who catches a psychotic sex-murderer, the "Lipstick Killer," will be named the firm's executive director.

The managers, who behave almost as cold-bloodedly as the murderer, lie and scheme to win the prize. In the end the diabolical son selects the only manager who schemes reluctantly. But the memory of director Fritz Lang's dark vision and of the devilish newspaper heir, who has only a "beautiful, faithless wife" to call his own, long outlives the movie's faux happy ending.

In recent decades, when the press triumphs, the owner lives offscreen, an invisible presence. *All the President's Men* features Jason Robards as Ben Bradlee, executive editor of the *Washington Post*, and Robert

Redford and Dustin Hoffman as the Hardy Boys of the newsroom, *Post* reporters Bob Woodward and Carl Bernstein. But owner/publisher Katharine Graham, whose support of the *Post*'s Watergate coverage Bradlee calls "state-of-the-art," remains a phantom.

In *The Paper* (1994), Graham Keighley (Jason Robards), publisher of the "New York Sun," makes only a cameo appearance at, significantly, a black-tie benefit. The "Sun's" city editor, Henry Hackett (Michael Keaton), worries that his penny-pinching paper will not report the likely innocence of two men accused of murder. "Not everything is about money," he tells Managing Editor Alicea Clark (Glenn Close). She snaps back, "It is when you almost fold every six months." Truth wins out, in part, one suspects, because the owner/publisher never deigns to stop by his near-death newspaper.

Increasingly, fiction and film replace the metropolitan newspaper with the superficial, suspect TV network as the institutional symbol of news. Ratings rule television news. Corporate bosses gut news operations to increase profits. In *Broadcast News* (1987), network chief Bill Rorish (Jack Nicholson) orchestrates the firing of 27 Washington bureau staffers as part of a $24 million cost cutting.

Integrity counts for a little. In the words of a character in Carole Nelson Douglas's novel *The Exclusive* (1986), "TV [is] no place for a journalist." People at WKRLD Channel 3 in Edward Gorman's *Murder Straight Up* (1986) kill a suicidal teenager to increase the impact of their teen-suicide series. In Paddy Chayefsky's *Network* (1976), the ratings of UBS-TV anchor Howard Beale (Peter Finch) spiral downward. Max Schumacher (William Holden), the experienced president of the news division, is fired to make way for Diana Christensen (Faye Dunaway), whom Schumacher accurately calls "television incarnate . . . indifferent to suffering, insensitive to joy . . . virulent madness." Christensen and other network executives huddle in a conference room to decide Beale's fate. Christensen asks, "What would you fellows say to an assassination?" Eventually network-supported terrorists assassinate Beale on camera.

In Chayefsky's view, the new corporate owners of the news media are more humanoid than human; they care nothing about news, the United States or democracy. "There is no America; there is no democracy," intones Arthur Jensen (Ned Beatty), the boss of the Communications Corporation of America (CCA), parent of UBS-TV. "There is only IBM and ITT and AT&T and DuPont, Dow, Union Carbide and

Exxon. Those are the nations of the world today." CCA will air any-thing likely to increase ratings and profits. "When the 12th-largest company in the world controls the most awesome, god-damned propa-ganda force in the whole godless world," Beale asks, "who knows what shit will be peddled for truth?"

CCA's chairman understands nothing about news. "I started as a salesman," he says. "They say I can sell anything." (Recently, the *New York Times Magazine* headlined an article about Italian media mag-nate Silvio Berlusconi, owner of three national television networks and a vast newspaper and magazine empire, "The World's Greatest Salesman." In real life perhaps, as in the movies, the values of journal-ism have given way to business's interest in selling more and increas-ing profits.)

Hollywood's antipathy toward media barons, often shadowy or in-visible figures, increasingly shapes its portrayal of all the press. And Hollywood's press is that shallow infotainment called, oxymoronically, television journalism. In the movies, anchors, station managers and other television journalists devalue and debase the news. Patrick Hale (Sean Connery), the television reporter in *Wrong Is Right* (1982) tells his boss: "And what about the killer I put on television. From death row to the electric chair. Fried meat on prime time. You paid $100,000 for that. Paid the killer. You call that journalism? We're in show business, baby. Make 'em laugh, make 'em cry, make 'em buy, by and by."

In killing the reporter, once a hero of movies, Hollywood further trashes the popular image of news media. And the Hollywood assault has its counterpart in novels. In Jeff Millar's *Private Sector* (1981), 200 giant corporations worldwide secretly conspire to buy the media to take over the U.S. government. The Consortium in Jack Anderson's *Control* (1988) and the EmpCom Holdings in Michael Thomas' *Hard Money* (1985) are equally avaricious international conglomerates in-tent on controlling U.S. news media. In David Aaron's *Agent of Influ-ence* (1989), Russian-subsidized French media mogul Marcel Bresson plots a takeover of America's most influential news media. Bresson warns: "Nations . . . are dangerously overarmed anachronisms. The earth will be ruled by global corporate organizations. And the key to global economic and political power is the media."

Now any human being associated with journalism—reporter, as well as owner—more often than not symbolizes civilization at its worst.

And as the size of conglomerate media owners grows, the worst goes global. So beware the rapacious rodent, that new global corporate media owner, Mickey Mouse.

Loren Ghiglione, a 1987–88 Media Studies Center fellow, is the former owner of Worcester County Newpapers. He is currently a professional in residence at The Freedom Forum's Newseum, curating an exhibit on New York newspeople, real and fictional.

8

Thinking Outside the Box

Christie Hefner

In the uncertain climate that defines life in communications industries today, experience can be an enemy. The more anyone has experienced, the more apt that person is to say, "Well, based on my experience, this is what the future will hold."

But today none of us knows what's around the corner. Consider the old analogy of blind men in a room feeling for an elephant, trying to figure out what it is. Now, given the high-tech nature of communications, it's not just blind men in a room with an elephant: The elephant is morphing.

For media industry leaders, one of the keys is a willingness to suspend confidence in your own knowledge. Then, as an extension of that, executives should foster a more participatory style of management. This is fairly critical in an unknown environment because you don't want people thinking, Well, let me figure out what the boss wants to know and that's what I'll say.

Leadership has to be collegial, so that people on the creative side and people on the distribution side and people on the marketing side and people on the research side and people on the finance side all interact more than they normally would. Collegial leadership won't eliminate the mistakes fostered by having a parochial perspective, but it should reduce them.

Now that so many media organizations have become very large and very complex, one style of leadership does not fit them all. (But then, I don't think that one style of leadership fits all situations in any circumstances.) You just have to look at your own organization to recognize that you're dealing with diverse people in a variety of situations—acknowledge that there isn't any one style that is equally effective over time, across all situations and for all people.

I sometimes get good ideas on leadership from reading, although I actually find that it can be more instructive to read a book about Abraham Lincoln during the Civil War than to read *The One-Minute Manager*. Biography and history and politics are more grounded in real-world leadership challenges. Books written about business and leadership that are not grounded in real-world challenges are frequently facile and superficial and, indeed, promote the idea that there is one style of leadership that works for everybody.

In leading a media conglomerate today, both the creative vision of an artist and the managerial skills of a businessperson are important. It's all about a blend of content and commerce. And in a media or entertainment company, one of the skills needed is the ability to create an environment in which creative people *want* to come to work and do their *best* work.

Often the kinds of qualities that a successful founder has are different from the set of skills required to manage at different times. But my own sense of the business world is that these skills are not polar opposites. It's not as if Ted Turner has no managerial business skills, or that someone like George Fisher has no creative skills.

At Playboy we're small enough (600 employees plus independent contractors like writers and directors) that it's possible for me personally to see leadership several layers down. Clearly, that must be harder in a much larger organization, where I imagine that what one would have to do as the CEO is rely on your president or your senior vice presidents or your vice presidents to help you identify leaders.

Gender is a factor in leadership styles, but there are as many leadership differences among women as there are differences between men and women. I've seen highly autocratic women leaders and I have seen very participatory, nurturing men leaders.

It's possible, and of some value, to talk in generalities about traditionally male or traditionally female qualities in leadership or executive ability, although that takes you down the road of traditional male qualities of aggressiveness and authority and traditional female qualities of participation. I used to say, with a chuckle, that those qualities of traditional female leadership and management never were valued until they got redefined as Japanese management styles—and then everybody thought they were very important!

But ultimately there is a wide range of styles of leadership within both sexes. And for all successful leaders and executives, the goal is to blend both of those kinds of abilities. You can paralyze an organization by having consensual management, and you can debilitate an organization, and the best people in it, if you are autocratic and dictatorial.

The entrepreneurial quality that a lot of trail blazers in the media businesses have, and the personal passion to take creative risks and to think outside the box, are as important as they ever were. Whether it's helping people outside your organization or trying to create an environment inside your organization, whatever benefits there may or may not be to scale, or synergy between distribution and creation, at the end of the day, it's the software, stupid.

_____

Christie Hefner is chairman and chief executive officer of Playboy Enterprises.

9

Concerns at the Top

Randall H. Lucius, Jeffrey A. Sonnenfeld and Michael Reene

Reporting on media mergers resounds with the voices of financial analysts, scholars, industry experts, journalists and regulators. Oddly underrepresented, however, are the perspectives of the people closest to these deals: Top communications leaders have been largely circumspect, as if they are afraid to draw the ire of regulators or the enmity of potential allies.

The scale of recent developments is astounding: Mergers in the media services segment of the information technology sector last year grew to a record 243, up 123 percent over the previous year. Yet the relative silence of industry leaders obscures the fact that media consolidation has created many strange new partnerships: horizontally integrated cable and telephone companies, vertically merged entertainment content providers and distributors, phone companies in information processing and entertainment ventures, and print publishers moving into electronic publishing. And while businesses converge, the mindsets of their leaders may not. The different media industry segments are not a monolith of values just because they have been linked by strategies and corporate charters.

An opportunity to survey executives from a variety of communications industries arose at the 1996 SuperComm Conference, sponsored by the Center for Leadership and Career Studies (CLCS) at Emory University. Since 1989, SuperComm has brought together representatives from the media, journalism, entertainment, publishing, telephony,

FIGURE 9.1
Mean Results by Industry to the Following Statement:
"The best way for an organization to succeed is to vertically integrate all
business processes from content to distribution."

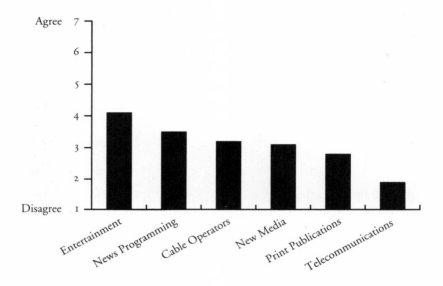

consulting, computer and government. Through computerized, interactive polling, as well as a detailed paper-and-pencil survey, the SuperComm 96 Conference survey collected 103 responses from executives in six main sectors of the communications industry: telecommunications, cable operators, entertainment, news programming, print publishing and new media. Our survey respondents were mostly between 40–49 years of age; the vast majority had 10 or more years of experience and held very high positions in their respective organizations, such as executive vice president and chief executive officer. Although the size of our sample has its limits, the answers we received in our survey raise important questions and possibilities.

We put to our conference participants questions to answer and statements to react to and then analyzed their reactions. One such statement was: "The best way for an organization to succeed is to vertically integrate all business processes from content to distribution."

FIGURE 9.2
Mean Results by Industry to the Following Statement:
"Company size stifles my organization's creativity."

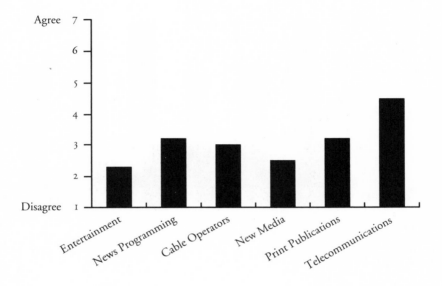

The responses we collected indicate that within a general climate of executive skepticism about vertical integration, the telecommunications executives were much more skeptical of vertical integration than others, particularly those from the entertainment industry. The entertainment executives' measured endorsement of vertical integration is consistent with the current trend of consolidation. While some analysts feel that the economic benefits of the merger boom are hard to discern economically, the entertainment industry insiders we sampled were more optimistic.

Telecommunications executives are more skeptical, but have nonetheless been active participants in the race to merge. The jury is still out on the value of many current telecom alliances, but worrisome examples abound. The Tele-TV venture owned by Bell Atlantic, Nynex and Pacific Telesis plans to spend $1 billion to buy set-top converter boxes, yet they still do not have a single customer. No one is sure

FIGURE 9.3
Perceptions of Organizational Flexibility by Industry

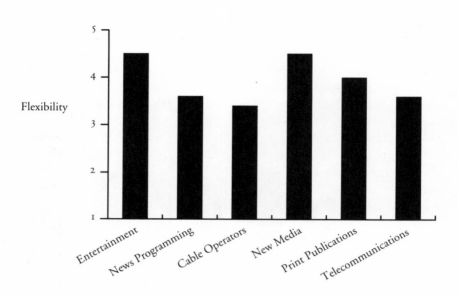

what the future holds for Americast, the interactive video joint venture formed by Disney, Capital Cities/ABC, GTE and four regional Bell companies.

Why are telecommunications executives more negative towards mergers? What do they know that other segments do not? Although the culture of industries within telecommunications is certainly unique in many respects, their experience, particularly with organizational size and bureaucracy, may provide valuable insight for other communication segments.

One process vital to industries such as entertainment, which may soon suffer at the hands of consolidation and increased size, is creativity. Many have preached the sermon that small is beautiful, believing that the creative process suffers at the hands of bureaucracy. Large manufacturing companies like 3M claim the key to their success lies in their loose, autonomous organizational structure, which resembles more a confederation than a bureaucracy. Far less, however, is known about the communications industry. And increased competition, along-side the seemingly endless advances in technology, has raised the value of creativity to an all-time high for survival.

The SuperComm 96 survey asked respondents to what extent they agreed or disagreed with the following statement: "Company size stifles my organization's creativity." The relationship between company size and the tendency to agree with the question was investigated first, and the larger their organization, the more likely executives were to agree that company size has stifled their organization's creativity.

A cross-industry perspective was used to determine if any measurable differences existed beyond the effects of company size. We found that industry differences play as much or more of a role in the attitudes toward creativity as the physical size of a company. Telecommunications executives signaled that in their organizations size had stifled creativity, whereas entertainment executives and new media executives did not feel that their company's size was influential.

Of course, entertainment and new media companies are significantly smaller than the telecommunications companies sampled for this study, but the recent entertainment mergers previously cited may soon change the dynamics of the entertainment business.

Since industry-specific factors independent of organizational size account for a sizable portion of the variance in attitudes towards size stifling creativity, cultural differences may exist between these companies. Our questionnaire included a series of values statements that reflect different types of organizational culture. Respondents were asked to rate the degree to which each value was encouraged or discouraged in their own company.

One cluster of statements dealt with the concept of flexibility, which is composed of such values as "adapting quickly to changes," "capitalizing on creativity" and "taking risks." Entertainment and new media executives endorsed items indicative of flexible cultures, but telecommunications executives did not. Flexibility, taken together with company size and industry type, further explains the variance in scores regarding attitudes towards creativity and appears to account for some of the variance between industries.

Overall, then, our results suggest that organizational size and cultural differences between industries both play a part in the discrepant attitudes towards vertical integration and creativity. Telecommunications executives are much less favorable about vertical integration than other segments of the communications industry, particularly entertainment. Telecommunications executives' experiences with large organizations and sizable bureaucracies could explain their skepticism towards integration, particularly with regard to creativity.

Entertainment, new media and other content creators depend on creativity for their survival. Entertainment and new media executives currently feel their creativity is unencumbered, but the significant results of size indicate that increasing company size diminishes creativity.

Beyond size, other factors unique to each industry exist. Cultural differences show that telecommunications companies are much less flexible than entertainment industries, which may be so for a number of reasons, such as historical or leadership factors. The nature of the telecommunications industry, where the delivery and distribution of content is more important than the content *per se*, certainly accounts for additional differences in the attitudes studied here. Nevertheless, size has an impact on attitudes towards creativity, independent of industry type or culture. Entertainment may be no more immune to the detrimental effects of increased size than any other branch of the communications industry. And because the size of many companies in communications will continue to increase, more inquiry into successfully stimulating creativity against the burden of growing size and complexity will be required and demanded by industry survivors.

Randall H. Lucius is research director at the Center for Leadership and Career Studies of the Goizueta Business School at Emory University and a Ph.D. candidate in psychology at the University of Georgia.

Jeffrey A. Sonnenfeld is professor of organization and management, and director of the Center for Leadership and Career Studies of the Goizueta Business School.

Michael Reene is vice president of IBM's Telecommunications & Media unit and general manager of telecommunications and media in the IBM Consulting Group.

IV

States of Media

10

Mergers, Word for Word

Susan Douglas and T. R. Durham

To understand media mergers, you must understand their terminology. As a public service, we present our readers with a glossary to help them grasp the true import of these momentous changes in medialand and its vocabulary:

NEW MANAGEMENT TEAM—a group of executives whose numbers are roughly equal to the population of Calcutta, whose combined salaries exceed the GNP of the United Arab Emirates and Japan, who oversee a newly merged company and whose job it is to produce synergy.

SYNERGY—*Current*: the transcendental, binding arc of energy that radiates throughout the land and all the peoples in it when two behemoths in the media industry seek to unite in order to clobber all known competition. *Obsolete*: oligopoly.

INFORMATION AGE—geologic epoch brought about by new management teams when human consciousness became glaciated by televentures and interactive on-line services, and people no longer had to leave their homes for anything.

CLUTTERED LANDSCAPE—industry with numerous upstart entities that actually participate in archaic market behavior once called "competition"; requires immediate branding and bundling.

BRANDING—using a corporate media logo made omnipresent by the annual expenditure of $17 billion to make an otherwise under-appreciated, generic infotainment service seem really special; a process indispensable to bundling.

BUNDLING—branding run amok, which leads to a plastering of the company name on every form of infotainment that the company can acquire. This strategic gambit to increase market domination immediately precedes unbundling.

UNBUNDLING—charging customers 37 times more than they once paid for a host of separate services that used to be included, sometimes even for free, in the bundle; accompanied by massive ad campaigns to persuade you that the newly unbundled bundle is not a leech on your wallet; required to support new management team synergizing the bundle.

WALL STREET REACTS POSITIVELY TO THE NEWS—Stock market gains 153 points as 100,000 workers are laid off.

INFOTAINMENT—1. unfairly maligned genre of television programming consisting of curvaceous models on exercycles who read the latest headlines while selling hair-care products. 2. style of television news now prevalent in the United States that guarantees the continued robust sales of blow-dryers and ensures that more Americans recognize the name Kato Kaelin than the names of their congressional representatives or senators.

FACTOIDS—electronically guided pieces of quasi-information made to swoop briefly through the mass consciousness before hurtling back out to rejoin Nebula Nebulorum.

DIGITAL SET-TOP BOX—device that will, by the year 2000, allow cable companies to offer 17,684 channels to their customers.

TO BE "DISADVANTAGED"—*Archaic*: to be a poor person suffering from inadequate educational resources, health care and job opportunities. *Current*: a company that failed to acquire a TV network, a cable company, a production studio, 40 AM and FM stations, an on-line service, a long-distance telephone company, orbiting satellites and the planet Jupiter.

VICE PRESIDENT FOR STRATEGIC PARTNERSHIPS—member of the management team who meets regularly with his counterparts in the two other companies dominating the global infotainment marketplace to see whose bundle is bigger.

GLOBAL ENTERTAINMENT COMPANY—a vertically, horizontally, diagonally and conglomerately integrated firm whose mission is to ensure that no yurt, no pueblo and no kraal is too small or too remote to receive "Home Improvement" or "Baywatch."

THE (CORPORATE NAME) "FAMILY"—how the CEO and management team refer to workers in the bundle to demonstrate their appreciation for the periodic sacrifices necessary for synergistic downsizing.

V-CHIP—electronic component that eliminates the need for government regulation and viewer choice, and which only 10–year-old boys will be able to program and operate. Also capable of transforming politicians into gibbering idiots without anybody noticing.

AUCTIONING THE AIRWAVES—the plan to return the airwaves to "the people" while simultaneously reducing the federal deficit by inviting prearranged bids from global multitainment companies striving to clean up the cluttered landscape and thus avoid becoming disadvantaged.

Susan Douglas, a professor of media and American studies at Hampshire College, is author of Where the Girls Are: Growing Up Female with the Mass Media *and* Inventing American Broadcasting, 1899 to 1922.

T. R. Durham, a former professor of business and economics, most recently at Skidmore College, is president of Durham's Tracklements, a purveyor of smoked foods.

11

Media Summits

Danny Schechter

Some years ago, when I was "dissecting" news on Boston's WBCN, a group of colleagues would get together every other week at what we dubbed the Shanghai Press Club, named after a Chinese restaurant on Boylston Street, to chow down, trade notes, commiserate, complain about our bosses and share ideas on stories we thought were important or uncovered. Our club disbanded after we worked our way completely through a rather expansive Szechwan menu.

A decade later when I became ensconced at ABC News, a group of us at different networks and outlets created the New York Media Forum as an irregular arena for debates on coverage issues. We networked while occasionally getting tipsy at the open bar that followed. Our goal, rare in our competitive business, was to find ways to connect, share experiences, collaborate and build a community.

The Shanghai Press Club and the New York Media Forum were both attempts to change the media from the bottom up. But today, in a world of mergers and media conglomerates, the really influential meetings are the ones that attempt to change the media from the top down— the expensive and exclusive conferences where high-level executives outline their corporate agendas, debate their visions and impress the men who prime the media money pumps on Wall Street. In an era of media empires, these gatherings are the new summit meetings, the get-togethers that have celebrated and, in some instances, fueled the transformation of the media landscape. They are the focus and source of

79

enormous power, settings where corporate media cultures congeal and sometimes collide. In panel discussions and informal conversations a certain "ideology fixing" takes place. Communications generals set the tone for the vast armies they command, unchallenged by critical voices or dissident perspectives. Yet for all their importance, these conferences form part of a media world not aggressively covered in the mainstream press.

All industries have their high-level conferences and Wall Street *soirées*. And among media bigwigs, industry associations and trade conferences are nothing new. But the media business, as one would expect, does it with panache. Top executives have many occasions for interacting: on panels, in fancy restaurants at the elite salons run by Colorado's Aspen Institute, at markets in Cannes or Los Angeles, at cable shows and NATPE (National Association of Television Program Executives) conventions.

Each summer, the most discrete and sought after of these affairs takes place at a ski resort in Sun Valley, Idaho, the home of investment banker Herb Allen, which he refers to somewhat coyly as a "summer camp." There CEOs mingle with financiers and assorted media moguls. Dealmaker Allen's role in a sense symbolizes the centrality of financiers in media decision-making in this era of rapidly changing technology and accelerated corporate concentration. It was there in 1995 that Michael Eisner of Disney and Thomas Murphy of Capital Cities/ABC decided to merge their companies in a $19 billion megamarriage. Warren Buffet, Cap Cities' principal investor, was on hand to help broker the deal that made one of America's richest men even richer. The commanding heights of Idaho served the commanding heights of media power as an out of the way, private venue, closed to the press and unwanted onlookers.

For the last six years each spring seems to bring on a summit for the media elite. The investment bank Schroder Wertheim & Co. Inc., teams up with the trade magazine *Variety* to stage an annual daylong conference, "The *Variety*/Schroder Wertheim Big Picture Media Conference," featuring many of the biggest names in the business behind show business. Journalism and commerce unite to bring an elite audience under one hotel ballroom roof—at $750 a pop—for a talkfest starring the scions of the American mediaocracy. (If there is a conflict here, no one speaks of it.)

The "Big Picture" brings together all the big men (and they usually are men) responsible for today's world of media-empire building. The annual meeting follows a conventional script with keynote speakers. Rupert Murdoch—for many years a controversial outcast in polite media company—was this year's headliner, introduced as the "Leader of the Media Industry." His text seemed to come from his annual report, laying out a map of his $9 billion global empire but first invoking a Ted Turnerism: "This business of being a 'buccaneer' isn't as easy as it looks." Murdoch went on to praise the FCC for "being more congenial to vertically integrated companies" and then launched into an upbeat and rather self-congratulatory talk about his deals, acquisitions and alliances worldwide. He only ducked one questioner, who asked about the state of his relationship with Communist China, where he removed the BBC from his STAR TV satellite because of Beijing's complaints about the BBC's human rights reporting. "No, I won't talk about that," he snapped. "I may get into trouble."

Many of the other panelists—who included NBC's Bob Wright, Cablevision's Charles Dolan, Hollywood producer Marcy Carsey and the now-unaffiliated Michael Fuchs (formerly chairman and CEO of HBO)—avoided contentious issues. They focused on problems facing the networks, cable, the telcos and direct broadcast satellite systems. When asked if the new media mergers will threaten creativity, Fuchs scoffed, "This is about profits, not about creativity." Carsey, the one person on the panel from the creative side, wasn't so sure.

Later in the day, there was a conspicuous absence of creativity when Westinghouse's Michael Jordan made what was billed as his first "major public address" since his company acquired CBS. Jordan's "vision" had little social content—he was enthusiastic about relaxing rules on station ownership while bragging about the "turnaround" he claimed he was responsible for at CBS. All the speakers dropped the latest industry buzzwords—"orbit slots," "augmented services," "MMDS," "platforms," "branding," "switched digital," "share shifting" and "enjoyment opportunities."

The presence of such a top-level cast testifies to the importance that executives attach to being seen at this event. "Most media executives operate in the valley," says Ivan Lustig, a Schroder Wertheim executive in charge of the conference, "and here's a chance for them to hear from people who are on the mountaintops and can tell them what's on the other side of the peak." The "Big Picture" provides a select audience a chance to ask questions from the floor and meet and greet high-level executives who are, most of the time, inaccessible. The most egalitarian place is the men's room where wannabes and wunderkids stand side by side.

None of the issues under discussion directly touch on news and public affairs, but they clearly do have a deep impact on the way television news has increasingly become a lower priority in this marketing-oriented environment. What *is* on the agenda is the state of business—how the digital age is here to stay, and how it will make a lot of people a lot of money, thanks to new technologies and the ability of well-positioned companies to exploit them. Peter Bart, *Variety*'s editor in chief, expressed reservations at the tenor of the sessions in the magazine's April 8–14 issue following the conference: In "Big Picture too rosy?" he deprecated an overemphasis on optimism and an underappreciation for candor and plain old humanity. He chided the speakers for referring to content—without, well, content.

The U.S. government also sends an emissary to remind these magnates that there is still a public interest to be served in the communications sphere. Reed E. Hundt, chairman of the Federal Communications Commission, has spoken with good humor and understated authority about the unfashionable notion that, in the end, the airwaves do belong to the people. At last year's "Big Picture" conference, Hundt invoked the forgotten memory of his predecessor, President Kennedy's FCC point person, Newton Minow, who became infamous 30 years earlier in the industry for describing television as a "vast wasteland." Hundt packaged his support for the public interest in self-interested terms. While lambasting so-called "*laissez-faire* extremists," he argued that the FCC is not the industry's enemy but in fact helps rationalize and stabilize the marketplace, saving them, in effect, from each other and themselves. This year, Hundt avoided all controversial issues and public interest advocacy—except for children—and instead appealed for help in reducing partisan bickering among the FCC commissioners, and support for "pragmatic policy-making."

At the '95 get-together, cable king Ted Turner did some good-old-boy bragging about the size and scale of his surging corporate portfolio. Between jokes about how hard it is to sit on uncomfortable chairs all day long and honest asides about how many of those present are really there to inflate their stock price, he forecast obliquely that the battle over the future of telecommunications in America, which plays itself out so politely on conference panels like these, will soon escalate in intensity. "It will get bloody before it is all over," he warned, giving no hint that he was then actively seeking to merge his company into a bigger entity, first sniffing around CBS, then courting NBC-GE, and, finally, seducing Time Warner in a merger that will, if it goes through, make him even more of a media powerhouse.

Also present last year was John Malone, the man who is, in many ways, the boss of America's media bosses. As a cable pioneer of pedigree, Malone said the future is "embedded in technologies." His speech was careful not to confuse "content" with conduit, focusing only on delivery systems as if it were obvious that the range of what we will have to watch is a given and that the values "embedded" in those systems are neutral. Clearly, they aren't, because it is the gatekeepers at the top who decide which services to offer and which to bag.

Despite the superficial bonhomie of the media summits, it is clear that most of the television network executives who appear, exuding self-confidence and the aura of power, are anything but "free." (Their lives and their humor were captured in an advertisement that ran this year in several broadcast trade magazines, featuring a quote from Hunter S. Thompson: "The TV business is a cruel and shallow money trench, a long plastic hallway where thieves and pimps run free and good men die like dogs." The ad added, "And there's also a negative side.") The executives who appear at conferences like "Big Picture" are forever constrained by the need to keep the next quarter's earnings up and to protect their backs in fierce internal politicking—known as "blood sports"—that breeds stress and insecurity. Michael Fuchs of HBO, was promoted just before last year's "Big Picture" conference (adding Time Warner's music division to his other portfolios) and fired not long after the conference. Nevertheless, he was back at the '96 event.

Howard Stringer, who rose from television news producer to CBS Broadcast Group president, has appeared regularly at the "Big Picture." In 1995, just after he had bailed out of Black Rock, he came to talk about his new interactive media venture. He was also one of the few panelist to speak in personal terms about how relieved he felt to get out of the pressure cooker. "It's great to be free," he later told the *New Yorker*. Freedom in the TV business usually means freedom to make more money, but Stringer actually offered a more idealistic vision, arguing that "interactivity . . . may be the magic that brings us together, crossing national boundaries faster than light—the social glue in the global village."

Stringer, now chairman and CEO of TELE-TV, was the only executive who spoke more broadly about how the technology and business issues that dominated the conference will affect society—and might have a beneficial effect for people worldwide. Missing from most of these meetings are voices to raise the issue of media accountability or to discuss how an increasingly concentrated industry will affect our political culture.

All of these media summits deserve better coverage in the mainstream press. At best, what is signaled at these events shows up first in the pages of industry trades like *Electronic Media* and *Variety* before it works its way into the popular press, if it ever does. Writers like Ken Auletta may deal with them in upscale magazines like the *New Yorker*, but the information very rarely trickles down. The erratic nature of such coverage is a problem because, increasingly, industry business is being done through informal networks—usually old-boys clubs—which surface at these relatively closed encounters. The business press does monitor media business transactions, but their analysis rarely incorporates a critical look at programming choices and priorities. Example: Why has so much money been invested in business news—hardly a mass-interest issue? Is this not just one more example of how the media ruling class reports on itself essentially for itself?

There will be more "Big Picture" conferences and events like them where the leaders of our most influential media enterprises sell their wares and themselves with amusing self-serving anecdotes, polite chatter and one-upmanship. In this world where hype rules, truth is often beside the point, and the existing coverage of "media bigs," to use an old *Variety*ism, does not necessarily provide accurate information. As Alan Citron, who has covered the business of entertainment for the *Los Angeles Times*, observed of the media beat: "There were a lot of occasions where I would interview a fairly powerful person and end up printing exactly the opposite after verifying the truth. . . . No one ever apologizes for not telling the truth."

The blend of news and show business that characterizes the "Big Picture" conferences does not make for searching discussions. In this vaunted "marketplace of ideas," the only idea *is* the marketplace—and how to dominate it.

Once, as I was observing all of this in well-fed arenas of high-powered chitchat, I flashed on Paddy Chayefsky's great movie of a generation ago about the amorality of the TV business. I then recalled

writer Michael Crichton's more recent comment about it: "A generation ago, Paddy Chayefsky's *Network* looked like an outrageous farce.
Today . . . *Network* looks like a documentary."

---

*Danny Schechter, a self-described "network refugee" (from CNN and
ABC News), is the executive producer of Globalvision Inc. and is
writing his media adventure story, "The More You Watch, The Less
You Know."*

12

The Buck Stops Here

The recent wave of media mergers has consolidated a vast amount of power and influence in the hands of an unprecedented few. The presidents, publishers and CEOs of huge conglomerates direct the operation of important newspapers, magazines, radio and television stations, and new media enterprises. As veteran journalist Walter Cronkite notes, "The buck stops with them. It's important that we know how they view their vast responsibility, for it is they who ultimately control our free press. It might be said that the press actually is as free as they permit it to be."

Because these companies are not just businesses but vital providers of news, the decisions made by the people at the top of the pyramid are extraordinarily important. In April 1996, Cronkite and the *Media Studies Journal* organized a roundtable discussion among several major media executives to explore their priorities and values in running their organizations and their responsibility for balancing the interests of business and news. The discussion was opened by Cronkite and moderated by Alex Jones, Pulitzer Prize winner, former *New York Times* media reporter and now host of the National Public Radio program "On the Media." Participating in the session were:

FRANK A. BENNACK JR., president and CEO of the Hearst Corp.
NEIL S. BRAUN, president of the NBC Television Network
P. ANTHONY RIDDER, CEO of Knight-Ridder Inc., and
ARTHUR OCHS SULZBERGER JR., publisher of the *New York Times*;

Excerpts of the discussion, which was also taped for broadcast use, appear below.

News and Profits

JONES: When you look at newspapers as a whole, my sense is that the wisdom in the newspaper industry these days is that we want to protect our profit margin; that's the top priority.

And that's being done by a reduction of newshole. A lot of newspapers got smaller this year. And I think that there is certainly a perception out there, maybe fed by the media critics, that something is happening to the newspaper industry that is making them charge more for fundamentally less.

SULZBERGER: I've only been a publisher for a few years, and I'd like to believe that the few years I have been a publisher are not going to be symptomatic of the years I have ahead, because I won't survive that experience. Because these have been very difficult years. We were hit, in 1987, with a market crash. . . . really, the worst recession in the newspaper business since the Great Depression. No sooner had that come to a close than we were hit by extraordinary newsprint price increases—our largest raw material cost just skyrocketed. And we're still in the middle or, at least I hope, at the end of that period.

The result has, not surprisingly, been that a lot of newspapers, a lot of newspaper owners, a lot of newspaper publishers have been trying to figure out where the hell to go: "What direction am I supposed to be taking this?"

Rule no. 1: No great newspaper has ever been an unprofitable newspaper, at least not for long. Rule No. 2: Investments in newsprint and newspaper technology are vastly more expensive than they were 20 years ago.

We just got the Edison plant up and running for about $360 million. It replaced a plant that we had built for $40 million.

Should we really be surprised that in all of those ups and downs, a lot of them being downs, we've had newsrooms feeling that they are under greater scrutiny and greater pressure than might have been true in the '80s, when money was flowing in at a much faster rate?

We shouldn't be surprised by that. We should expect that. But I think what you need to look at is the actual quality of the news that's available to people. I mean, you can second guess people backwards and forwards, but there are first-rate newspapers out there today.

JONES: Well, a first-rate newspaper in New York, New York *Newsday*, arguably a very, very good product, was killed. It was done for reasons that made perfect sense in a corporate sense and made no sense if your values had to do with being a citizen of New York and wanting to have access to the news report that that creature provided.

RIDDER: But does Times Mirror have an obligation to continue to lose money because some people in New York would like to read another newspaper? I mean, there are a lot of choices in New York.

JONES: You see, Tony, that's exactly what I'm trying to get at. Where is the line between making a lot of money, breaking even, acceptable profit? That is what your job is—to decide.

SULZBERGER: Your question is, How high is high? What do we consider an acceptable profit? And I think every one of us would answer that differently. That's our job. Our job is to balance that.

BENNACK: I can't tell you where the line that you're looking for gets drawn. But I do want to give you a response that I think is relevant.

The line gets drawn where there is an inability to attract capital. That's true of all businesses. Now, in the newspaper business—I think more maybe than other media, but in all business—ultimately there has to be a return on capital. The culture of these companies that are in the newspaper business and the histories of the people who run them means that there's a higher commitment to being in this business than the pure return on capital.

But you can't repeal the law of economics. And if you look at the recent track record, the return on equity of media businesses, which everyone thinks of as very glamorous businesses, and they are, has grown through our lifetimes. Nonetheless, the return on equity of many of the companies we're talking about today fall below the return on equity of the industrial complex at large. . . .

I'm not sure the general public recognizes this, but the people who work in and own and manage businesses, newspapers, broadcasting stations, etc., are terribly in love with those businesses and have a devotion to reinvestment and to expanding that often doesn't defy economics but has little to do with economics.

The objectives are, of course, profit-oriented, and capital has to be attractive. If Arthur is going to build a $350 million plant, that money has to come from somewhere. So I think the answer, as a generalization, is that if you're in a market situation or in an industry that can no longer attract capital competitively, you have a problem.

* * *

BRAUN: You asked me before, why are we spending all this money on msNBC? It's because we have a mission to be as profitable as we can. But we have another mission. And that's to be the pre-eminent leader in news coverage. We want people, when they turn on their televisions for whatever story is happening in the world, we want them to come to NBC first because that's the authoritative source.

That's where they're going to get the fastest reporting, the most objective reporting and the most insightful reporting. And I don't think that's ever going to change. And I think there's always going to be a huge demand for that product, whether it's in print, whether it's electronic or whether it's broadcast.

* * *

JONES: Do you feel that Wall Street has taken some of your discretion away, simply because of the pressure you're feeling? Discretion about how you decide about resources, things you might do that you don't do?

SULZBERGER: You can't do everything in a given year. I think your question is, how much of an impact do we have to make one year better than the next year financially? And the answer is—absolutely, that's there.

We all want to see growth. We want to see growth in our journalism, and we want to see growth in our profitability. Have there been times we've postponed decisions to another year so that we don't have to bear the expense of it? Absolutely. Yes, there have been those times. Have there been times when we've actually not done something we thought we needed to do for the business? Never.

And that's the adjustment you have to make. In the end we're all in this for the long-term. In the end that means we're going to have to assure our customers—our readers and our advertisers—that they're getting a newspaper or newspapers that they want to read, want to advertise in.

That drives our thinking; it drives my thinking more than any other single fact. The rest then just has to be balanced according to what you can swallow, according to what your needs are for that year financially.

If another part of the company is going to have a very good year, that helps the *New York Times* newspaper, perhaps, to take on a little more expense. If the reverse is the case, and it looks like the *New York*

Times will be driving company earnings, well, then maybe we'll back off from some of our expense items to keep that number higher.

* * *

JONES: You are the head of a company that does not have the scrutiny from Wall Street that these other gentlemen have to endure. How much of a skewed element, in terms of decision making, do you think that is, versus what Hearst imposes on itself?

BENNACK: Well, I would be less than honest if I didn't tell you that it's a significant benefit. . . I think probably the largest benefit is the absence of public quarterly reporting, because there are very few things that can be started at the beginning and finished by the end of a single quarter.

BRAUN: But, to sort of make the opposite-end-of-the spectrum argument, I mean, being part of such a large company—the second-largest capitalized company in the world, GE—what we spend in news or don't spend in news is immaterial to the profitability of General Electric.

And because General Electric is such a high profile, high visibility, always-in-the-public-scrutiny type of company, the last thing GE would want to do is something that was going to draw the ire of every journalist . . . I would make the argument that simply because of our size and because of our profile, our corporate parent bends over backwards not to be perceived as cutting budgets or news capabilities.

* * *

JONES: Tony Ridder, let me ask you to help us define the job of CEO and chairman of Knight-Ridder by talking about what you can't do—what a man in your position, with the company and the power that you have, is not able to accomplish that you might want to, within the company framework?

RIDDER: I wish I could spend more time out in the field, because one of the really fun parts of a job like mine is to spend time with people.

One of the things that I don't do, that I guess I could do but would never do, is get involved in setting the editorial policy of any of our newspapers. The editorial decisions that appear on the editorial pages are all made by our local publishers and editors. . . .

Our newspapers serve regions or local communities, and people that live and work in those communities know best what works for that community. So I don't think somebody sitting in Miami ought to decide what's best for Philadelphia or Detroit or San Jose.

JONES: But part of your job in Miami is making decisions that affect Charlotte and Detroit and Philadelphia and other places where you have great newspapers. And you've been beaten up in the press, especially in the journalistic press, in the last couple of years, because there's a perception that Knight-Ridder is changing the way it looks at that balance between business priorities and news priorities. . . .

Is it not a valid argument that Knight-Ridder is doing something that could jeopardize those news reputations?

RIDDER: I don't accept the fact that it's going to jeopardize the news judgments or the quality of the newspapers. And it's interesting that in Philadelphia, which probably has been written about more than any other place, there's a case where we are trying to double the profit margins because their profit margin last year was below 8 percent; it was about 7.5 percent.

And we're trying to move that profit margin in '97 up to the mid-teens and maybe even higher. So there is a case where it's double. But we have many newspapers that are operating in the 20s and we're not necessarily trying to move their margins at all. . . .

There's always been a certain amount of tension between corporate and people in the field. And the corporate staffs in our business tend to want more profit than the newspapers are prepared to give. I mean, I know what it felt like from the other side.

It is interesting to me that people are writing about it now as if it's some new phenomenon that didn't even exist before.

I am the chairman and chief executive officer, and before that I was president of the newspaper division and president of the company. When I was president of the newspaper division, I used to sit in on a lot of the budget meetings. . . . to make sure that the editors felt comfortable with what was going on.

JONES: Do you really expect them to tell you if they don't?

RIDDER: I'll tell you, Knight-Ridder editors are not shy.

Feedback

RIDDER: I think it's important to realize that we have five constituencies and our shareholders are just one of five constituencies. So it's our employees, it's our customers, our advertisers and our readers, and it's serving our communities as well.

Our job is to balance those constituencies and I think many times people think, Oh, there's only one constituency they care about and that's the shareholders.

JONES: How do representatives of these other constituencies approach you? How do they penetrate the sort of corporate cocoon that you necessarily live in a fair amount of the time? How does that get cracked so that you are open-mindedly presented with a perspective that you may not agree with?

When you read these critical articles, not just about Knight-Ridder but about the industry, does it make any impression?

RIDDER: Well, I wouldn't say it's discounted. I think a lot of it is very painful, quite frankly. But I think a lot of it is what I would call—whining. A lot of it is inaccurate but it hurts. It's painful.

SULZBERGER: I wish there was more of a cocoon sometimes than you seem to think there is. I can't, I won't, speak for my colleagues, but I feel wonderfully accessible. And whenever you're at the top of an organization, be it at the newspaper or a company, you're going to be a free target for shots. That's okay, that's our business. We give people shots, too. So we better have a thick enough skin to take it when it's our turn to take shots.

Sometimes it hurts, but, look, there's a real easy way to find out if things are going significantly wrong. Your advertisers stop advertising and your readers stop reading.

So if you start to look and a circulation declines and there's nothing else out there that will help you ascertain what's going on—you haven't had big price increases recently, for example . . . then you've got to make the assumption that you're doing something wrong. The readers are telling you that this isn't enough anymore. It's the marketplace.

Newspapers for New Times

JONES: Many newspapers are perceived to be putting their investment in their profit margins, instead of preserving and enhancing the product itself. Do you think that's true, as you look broadly?

SULZBERGER: I don't have the information to say whether that's true or not. I can speak to what we're doing at the *New York Times*, but I don't know what the books look like at other newspapers and other newspaper companies.

I suspect they're struggling with the same thing we're struggling with, which is how to redefine ourselves in an era where information is being segmented.

And some information is becoming generic that never before was generic news. Information that you can get from a dozen different sources and therefore has become less and less valuable. There's not a lot of money to be made in that kind of news. The other half of that equation is value-added news—the news that newspapers and magazines are uniquely equipped to collect, to process and to report back to our readers, and which you can charge a lot of money for.

And that's a challenge we're facing at the *Times*. I suspect it's a challenge that every newspaper company is facing right now.

New Media, New Journalism

SULZBERGER: There's something coming down the pike which is interesting and that leads to a lower cost of distribution. And it is the Internet. The Internet, in my judgment, while it's going to be some years before it's a huge success, offers us a way of distributing our information at tremendously low costs. No more worrying about pricing on paper.

No more worrying about trucking costs. No more worrying about printing and distribution in the broadest sense. When that happens— and it's conceivable that it will happen 10, 20 years from now—and that becomes a very viable medium for distributing information, then we're really only building our business on the back of our journalism.

JONES: You know, one of the things that seems to be taking shape as it evolves is that it's going to put the *New York Times* and every Knight-Ridder newspaper and every Hearst newspaper and NBC and every other major news organization in the country in direct competition with each other. . . .

BRAUN: Yes and no, Alex. Yes, in the sense that we will all be available to the consumer across the same medium, the same box, if you will. But no, in the sense that the *New York Times* newspaper won't be giving you the news about Houston and the way to live your life in Houston.

JONES: Can the *Houston Chronicle* be sure that it is going to be the dominant local news gatherer there?

BENNACK: No, absolutely not. It can't be sure. It's an effort that must be made each and every day. However, with the kind of attention that I would hope we can bring to it, the preservation of being the leading provider is achievable.

But the word "dominant" is probably a non sequitur in a world that is as fragmented and as changing as this one is.

The newspaper business and print publications cannot be solely dependent on ad revenues. I think there must be participation, an appetite, a desire to receive them by their audiences, or they lose their reasons for being, not to mention having an economic equation that is not sustainable. . . . Over time, it is my view that readers will pay a heavier share of the total cost of the product than they do today or than they did yesterday.

BRAUN: Business can be very constructive here. The fact is that there's such a multiplicity of voices now, it makes the common, shared experience more difficult. But the individual choice of where you get your information—and who presents it to you and in what context and depth of analysis—is growing geometrically.

From a consumer point of view, from a First Amendment point of view, the opportunity to hear a multiplicity of voices is driven by technology, and it's not driven by profits and losses at this company.

We're an affiliation of 215 local stations. Our competitive advantage against other media is that we have a strong local identity through our stations. And we have a strong national and international identity through the network. And the combination of big and local is what we bring to the viewer's home.

* * *

JONES: Frank, your Hearst Corp. is in everything in a big way. You sort of cover all bases here. When you look ahead, where do you see the area where you want to put your resources when it comes to investing for the future?

BENNACK: We have made a significant investment in newspapers over the past decade, with the acquisition of the *Houston Chronicle*, for example.

We are approaching an equal distribution in our company between electronic media and print media, even though Hearst is obviously best known as a newspaper publisher.

Television, Business and Journalism

JONES: The three major networks are now all owned by gigantic conglomerates that are not really directly involved in the news business at all, at the highest levels. . . .

BRAUN: First of all, let me fundamentally challenge your premise that business and journalism are fundamentally at odds. I think good business and profitability and good journalism can be complementary objectives, and the fact that you spend less money in a moment in time does not necessarily say that the quality of your news reporting is going down.

And you have to look at what you're doing over a period of time. In the investment we've just made jointly with Microsoft to create a whole new way of providing news content to consumers—we're trying to say that if broadcast news has historically been headlines and has been relegated more to a headline position because you now have linear coverage on a CNN, what's the next evolution of content providing? We think it's multimedia.

So we're going to have a single-branded news product that will come from NBC. We'll have a cable channel that follows things on a linear basis. And we'll also have an on-line Web site component that will be able to give you all the background in history, if you want to go deeper into the information, all cross-promoted, all cross-referenced.

And we're making a huge financial commitment. I will tell you categorically that the projected break-even on that enterprise is way beyond what any financial analyst would accept. You couldn't get a Wall Street or venture capitalist to make this investment.

V

The Consequences of Media
Empires in the United States

13

Corporate Journalism and
Community Service

Gene Roberts

One of the most vivid images I carry in my mind from my editing years in Philadelphia is of a photograph taken in the legislative chamber of the Pennsylvania State Capitol in Harrisburg. Voting by electronic lever is taking place, and one legislator obviously wants the vote to go his way. The picture shows him flat on his belly, spread-eagled across several desks. He is voting four times. His hands are pushing two levers. His feet are pushing two more.

I think of this picture often as it becomes clear that more and more regulatory and monetary control is being pushed out of the federal government and onto state and local governments. Some of these governments are so bad as to defy belief. Some are as good as it may be possible for any government to be. But good or bad, state and local governments are becoming vastly more important and significantly more newsworthy.

This, as a result, should be a heady time for state and local newspapers. But it is not. Many, perhaps most, of these newspapers are weaker in staff, newshole and commitment to governmental coverage than they have been in decades. A tragedy may be in the making for journalism and for democracy.

Much of the problem can be traced to changes in the ownership patterns of newspapers. It is no secret that American newspapers increasingly have come under control of corporate chains—many of them publicly held and solicitous of Wall Street analysts who see no newspaper obligations other than the bottom line. Not all chains fail to meet their journalistic obligations, of course, nor do all independent owners meet them. But chain ownership has become so pervasive that giant corporations pipe the tune to which most of journalism marches.

Seventy-five percent of America's dailies are now in the hands of chains. Seventy-four percent of this nation's state capitals are served— or ill-served—by chains. And large chains are gobbling up the small ones. Just four of the chains—Thompson, American, Gannett and Donrey—own 21 percent of all of the nation's daily newspapers in the United States. Put another way, four chief executive officers control more than one-fifth of the nation's dailies.

Chains and groups will tell you they don't interfere with local coverage, they simply insist that each newspaper return an "acceptable" level of profits to the central corporation—even when the economy is bad or newsprint prices soar. This alone is enough to cause newspapers, which are cyclical businesses, to weaken their coverage by slashing newsholes and newsroom staff. But there are problems even beyond these.

News coverage is being shaped by corporate executives at headquarters far from the local scene. It is seldom done by corporate directives or fiat. It rarely involves killing or slanting stories. Usually it is by the appointment of a pliable editor, by a corporate graphics conference that results in a more uniform look or by the corporate research director's interpretation of reader surveys that seek simple common-denominator solutions to complex coverage problems.

Often the corporate view is hostile to governmental coverage. It has been fashionable for some years, during meetings of editors and publishers, to deplore "incremental" news coverage. Supposedly, it is boring, a turn-off to readers, and—what's worse—it requires newshole. The problem with all of this is that governmental news develops incrementally. And if you don't cover it incrementally, you don't really cover it at all. Incremental is what it is all about. Someone introduces a bill or an ordinance. It goes to a committee. The committee accepts it, rejects it or amends it. It goes to the floor. There is usually debate, amendment attempts, voting. And if it passes, it often must be signed or vetoed by a governmental executive, in the case of a state by a governor. Keeping incremental coverage interesting is a problem. But we have solved it by dropping the coverage rather than by working hard to make it readable and enticing.

Governmental news may not be as gut-wrenching as rape, murder, airplane crashes and other mayhem. But many of our most serious readers take it seriously. It is the way—virtually the only way—they have to keep up with what is going on in government. And if newspapers miss a step along the path of legislation, then readers also miss a step and don't get to weigh in at the proper time.

Supplying this part of the news fills a basic need of democracy. Being able to present it fully and without fear of censorship is, of course, one of the reasons the First Amendment has taken on such importance in our society. But freedom comes with obligations. And the obligation of the press is, at its heart, very simple: supplying voters with the information they need to make decisions in our democracy.

Substantive news coverage is not only vital to democracy; it is vital to the survival of newspapers. As papers become increasingly shallow and niggardly, they lose their pertinence to their readers and their communities. And that is ultimately suicidal.

If newspapers want to survive they absolutely must pay more attention to their serious and most devoted readers. But most newspapers are worrying about the casual or marginal reader to the neglect of the serious reader. They cut back on jumps of stories off Page 1. They run photographs and graphics simply because they are colorful, not because they are newsy or have human interest value. They opt for froth over information. This is nutty.

People who want more detail, who want more stories from which to choose, are our hard-core readers and are the most important insurance a newspaper has. Each time we restrict these readers' options by cutting back on staff and newshole, we cut back on our insurance. We become more vulnerable—and less essential.

Why is it so difficult for the managers of newspapers to grasp this? Again, part of the answer is the corporatization of newspapers. Most newspaper chains tie the compensation of their managers and editors to annual profits. Go down in profits in a given year and your compensation falls—sometimes very sharply. Go up in profits and you are rewarded—sometimes very handsomely. Put three very profitable years together and the chain promotes you from publisher of a newspaper of 25,000 circulation to one of 50,000. Is it any wonder that newspaper managers make short-term decisions to the long-term detriment of newspapers?

But it isn't as easy to make profit goals today as it was in the 1960s and '70s and early '80s. When I entered the newspaper business in the mid-1950s, newspaper technology was not that much different than when my father entered it 25 years before me. In the late 1950s, however, technological improvements began exploding their way into newspapers. Hot type disappeared over a 25 year period, and entire composing rooms, stereotype and engraving departments vanished.

In this environment newspapers could buy additional papers, enact efficiencies by applying what they had learned from one paper to another, increase profits and still have money left over to improve newsrooms and increase newshole. Many formerly independent papers actually got better.

Today, however, production efficiencies have been made on most papers, and there is more competition for advertising dollars. For some time, corporations have been faced with two choices: one, accept that they are cyclical businesses with profit levels that will go up and down with the local economy and with newsprint prices; or two, paper over economic pressures by squeezing newsroom staffs, budgets and newshole. Too many papers, alas, are choosing the latter course thus imperiling their futures.

The trends for most newspapers are dismayingly clear. They are turning their backs on news and comprehensive coverage—the very things that made them community institutions and valuable properties in the first place. Editors and news staffs are becoming disenchanted, disheartened and disillusioned.

With a few exceptions, the talk at the high levels of newspapers these days is of increasing profits, increasing corporate pressure, increasing responsibility to shareholders. Almost never is there talk of the financial commitment necessary to live up to our communities and our nation. To talk of increasing coverage or newshole or staff on most newspapers now would be tantamount to confessing lunacy. And that is a tragedy—because sound, readable, dependable news coverage *is* our future.

It is time, high time, that newspaper corporations become subjects of debate and be held accountable for covering the communities they serve. Meanwhile, many are managing their newspapers like chain shoe stores, with no sense of being important community institutions with highly important responsibilities to the public.

Gene Roberts is managing editor of the New York Times *and former executive editor and president of the* Philadelphia Inquirer. *This essay is adapted from "Corporatism vs. Journalism: Is It Twilight for Press Responsibility?" delivered as the Press Enterprise Lecture at the University of California at Riverside, Feb. 12, 1996.*

14

The Big News-Big Business Bargain

Tom Wolzien

In these days of media mergers, controversies over the CBS and ABC tobacco stories raise four critical questions for television news. Is there an inherent conflict of interest between news divisions and their larger corporate parents? Are the motives of news organizations or corporate managers who decide against their reporting teams suspect? Are corporate decisions regarding news driven by concerns over the price of the parent company's stock? Are corporate acquisitions of media enterprises bad because they cause companies to place journalistic principles on hold pending completion of the sale?

These issues are not new. As a street reporter, as an executive producer, as a member of news and corporate management, and now as a Wall Street analyst of media companies, I've been involved in attacks by companies or individuals who didn't like a story, in decisions whether to retract stories and in efforts to gauge the impact of threatened lawsuits on the value of stocks. And I've concluded that in an era of corporate mergers and multibillion-dollar lawsuits, big news needs big business. Who else can afford the risks or the cost of catastrophic libel insurance with its multimillion-dollar premiums and $5 million deductibles? At issue is not whether there will be a corporate parent, but the integrity and size of the corporate parent.

The romantic image may be an ink-stained local news person fighting the forces of small-town evil, but the reality is that newspeople making six- and seven-figure salaries are frequently corporations themselves. They practice journalism as subcontractors of still larger corporations, which themselves are owned by yet bigger corporations, which are usually owned by public shareholders—principally the mutual and pension funds where many of those very newspeople (and readers of this article) have some of their life savings.

Alone, television news organizations are not big enough to withstand the legal threats of huge, entrenched industries like tobacco or oil. Even a company the size of pre-Westinghouse CBS, with a stock market value of some $5 billion, could have been bankrupted by a jury award of the amount sought in some recent cases.

Yet as scary as the prospect of such libel awards may be, the real incentives for a bargain between big business and big news lie more in the economics of network news. Depending on its prime-time operations and ratings, a typical network news division sees between a $50 million profit and a $50 million loss. When depreciation for capital equipment (cameras, tape machines, computers, studios) is subtracted, even what initially looked like a money-making broadcast network news operation may actually see a loss. And when taxes and interest on debt to buy the building and the equipment are added along with corporate administrative costs and insurance, the result is hardly something that most people would want to buy stock in for their retirement. Such a business, furthermore, would easily be damaged by just the legal fees of a major lawsuit. For all these reasons, there are no stand-alone, publicly traded television network news operations. The economics don't justify it.

In fact, the economics no longer justify stand-alone broadcast networks, whose profitability has declined as viewers zap around to a wide assortment of cable offerings. With more choices, the revenue pie gets split among more players, the costs of holding onto viewers climb, and networks have had to become part of still larger companies.

Now networks and their news organizations are part of companies worth tens of billions of dollars. At the post-merger ABC television network, the total profits of the news division are only 1 percent of the entire Disney company. That means that news is not financially material to the whole company. And that may give the news division some freedom in dealing with major investigative pieces. Where a lawsuit may be big, the company's resources are bigger. In a world of big-time news risks, only the largest of corporate parents have the resources to tolerate the risk.

As parent companies get bigger, the rules will change for newspeople. Reporters will need to be more precise. Precision is essential to protect against attack, even though viewers probably don't care if the assembly sequence for a product goes from A to Z rather than from Z to A, as a story might have reported. Of course, it has always been the responsibility of a newsperson to get the story right, but in the past minor errors often escaped notice. Today if a story isn't right, if it is off by only one substantive detail, then that's the opening that the attacked corporation needs to destroy the whole piece, no matter how correct it otherwise might have been. And with larger corporate parents who themselves are sensitive to precision in reporting about their own company, any hint of error will dissipate corporate support faster than anything short of the appearance of a cover-up.

Yet if the story is correct in all its details, then the issue becomes the resources and resolve of the corporate parent. A good corporate parent understands the trade of the risks of news for the rewards of ownership of a national news operation—image, access to just about everyone in Washington and through that access political clout on issues of importance to the corporation. Big companies build leverage off their news division's ability to fill the Kennedy Center with every politician in Washington for a political debate—and then have their lobbyists work the aisles. Heads of companies that own national news operations get more than their share of invitations to small affairs at the White House and meetings with heads of state.

Corporations owning big news operations don't need to skew the news on the air. To the contrary, the power that accrues to the corporate parent of a news operation comes from the independence of that news operation. Without such integrity, neither party will be taken seriously.

A bad corporate parent—one whose top executives are unwilling to accept the occasional risks of news in exchange for these benefits—will sell out a news operation at the first sign of adversity. But this has nothing to do with bigness or mergers. Few of us who have been in the business for an extended period haven't watched a station manager or small publisher take a dive under advertising pressure.

Journalists themselves may have more indirect clout with a very large publicity-conscious corporate parent. The larger the organization, the more connected its journalists are with those at other big media companies, and the more likely the fraternity of news will rally around any suspicion of sell out. (Thus Larry Grossman's exceptional *Columbia Journalism Review* piece on the "60 Minutes" case, and the wide coverage of both the ABC and CBS controversies in print and broadcast.)

The news fraternity is the best protection for news operations within new and ongoing corporate ownership structures. Big companies are adverse to bad publicity—and the bigger the company, the more adverse. They are adverse to their top officers appearing to be going against the public good. And they are, ultimately, more vulnerable to the pressure of image than the threat of legal action.

The operative word in the last paragraph is "ongoing." When something is being sold, there is no telling what a management may do to protect a deal. Of course, there's no telling how many termite holes you might paint over to enhance the value of your house when you sell it. There is no way for me to judge whether punches were pulled to protect a sale of CBS or ABC. This may sound like a cop-out, but having been involved in a number of internal investigations of stories which were challenged, I know that unless you are the one questioning the principles, reviewing each frame of tape, talking with the lawyers and taking apart each claim by the opposition, you are not in a position to make a reasoned judgment on the accuracy of a story or the need for settlement. Even with this access, reasonable professionals may differ. And of course in news, as in life, it is easy to be righteous about the decisions of others.

Do threatened lawsuits affect the price of the stock of the parent of a news organization? I've seen no evidence of this. No client from a large pension or mutual fund has ever told me he was worried about the impact of a threatened lawsuit over a news story, and I have not advised him to worry. There are several reasons. First, because the investment horizon for most funds is six to 24 months, and most lawsuits take nearly a decade to ride all the way through the Supreme Court, the risk of immediate financial impact on a company's stock is remote. Second, all big media companies carry business catastrophe insurance, so even if the company eventually lost the case, the actual liability is limited to the deductible plus the amount beyond the coverage. Third, there is a reasonable presumption on the part of investors that news organizations will be professional and retract, apologize and settle when they have made a mistake. If news organizations so police themselves then the courts will continue to be fair in awards, and media companies will not be bankrupted. And fourth, most savvy media investors understand that plaintiffs are trying to support their own stock prices by making wild initial claims for damages.

All this may help explain why Disney Chairman Michael Eisner selected his shareholder meeting—where the Cap Cities merger was approved—to focus on the need for both the support of and independence of ABC News. It may explain why Westinghouse and the new management at CBS rolled out the "60 Minutes" tobacco story shortly after the merger. And it may explain why GE and NBC News appear to have reached *détente* and mutual understanding after early years of misjudgments on both sides.

Huge corporate parents and their news divisions appear to be entering into a mutually supportive bargain, in which newspeople will deliver accurate stories and receive the support of corporations that understand the status and intangible benefits of owning a news organization. But if one side doesn't live up to the bargain, there will be penalties. Corporate managers who take a dive on a story must expect the news fraternity to rally with heavy adverse publicity. Such managers may find their image damaged in Washington and investors questioning the quality of their judgment. And newspeople who do not deliver precision in controversial stories will be corrected quickly if they don't correct themselves. If they try to cover up, their news organizations will be exorcised as NBC News and "Dateline" were after the GM truck incident.

Tom Wolzien, a media analyst with Sanford C. Bernstein & Co., was senior vice president of cable and business development and a news producer at NBC.

15

The Homogenization of Hollywood

Barbara Maltby

Japan's late 20th-century investment in Hollywood prompted fear of a foreign takeover of an engine of American culture. Those fears, based on Japanese colonization of two of the six major studios, turned out to be short-lived. Neither Sony nor Matsushita changed the structure of Hollywood moviemaking, nor kidnapped the (Hollywood-style) American dream. Sony simply pushed the culture of Hollywood, which rests on a foundation of money, power and ego, to indulge in new excesses.

Now Hollywood is in the midst of another anxious evolution, as studio and independent production companies are swallowed up by huge vertically integrated monoliths like Viacom (Paramount), News Corp. (Fox), Disney (ABC) and the projected combination of Time Warner and Turner, which itself owns Turner Pictures, Castle Rock, New Line Pictures and Fine Line Productions. Yet, rather than change the way movies are made, these mergers are merely going to accelerate a transformation already under way toward greater emphasis on the bottom line, more homogenization of content and less risk taking. Such forces were already at work in Hollywood before a fit of mergers seized the film industry.

Hollywood has always been an uneasy mix of art and commerce. The creative process is a messy one, by its very nature individual and unpredictable, recalcitrant in the face of programming and control, even in the form of contractual obligations. Only one out of maybe

111

every 50 to 100 projects that is put into development actually gets made. The slog toward the Bethlehem of an actual start date, a process referred to as "development hell," can take anywhere from three to 10 years.

While artistically successful movies tend to be the result of a writer's or director's passionate and idiosyncratic vision, the business of Hollywood wants reliable "product" that will make a lot of money by attracting large audiences. (Films are actually referred to as "product," as in "Columbia doesn't have enough product in its pipeline.") Tension has always existed between moviemakers' desire for creative freedom and relentless studio pressure to make the product—whatever its artistic or social pretensions—conform to current models of what target audiences seem to want. In the 1980s that target audience was American males aged 14–25; hence the flood of increasingly violent, indistinguishable action-adventure movies. Today the target audience is international, and the mainstay of the market turns out to be these same action-adventure movies whose formulaic plotlines cross cultural boundaries.

Hollywood must attract mass audiences because movies have become incredibly expensive to produce. Talent, thanks to the precedent set in the '80s by high-powered agencies like Michael Ovitz's Creative Artists Agency, has grown much more expensive. High union costs, special effects and a general tendency towards major excess also contribute to increasing the cost of producing and marketing a movie to an average of $60 million.

As costs rise, profits become more difficult to realize. Hollywood's double-entry "creative" cost accounting, made infamous by Art Buchwald's lawsuit over *Made in America*, coupled with the tendency to woo big stars and directors with a percentage of gross revenues, has created the "rolling break-even"—a point of profit that always seems just beyond reach. *Forrest Gump* has made an astronomical $650 million dollars but, astonishingly, Paramount says that the movie still hasn't broken even.

Not surprisingly, less than one third of all movies turn a profit. Megahits are needed to fill the coffers *and* underwrite those losses. Today it is not enough for a film to make money in this country, even with ancillary sales to cable, video and other outlets. It must also play well overseas.

The problem for studio executives is that even a reliance on seemingly tried-and-true formulas can't guarantee a hit. No matter how precise the demographic studies or how aggressive the marketing campaign, audience taste is unpredictable and transient—witness the monumental failure of *The Last Action Hero*. It is a Hollywood Truism that no one can ever be sure what will be a hit; at best, there are only educated guesses.

That uncertainty breeds pervasive fear because *so* much money is at stake, money that provides both profits for the corporate parent and underwrites the "Hollywood life-style" that sustains fragile and uneasy egos. No wonder studio executives avoid making small, artistically unique films with seemingly limited audience appeal. In their timidity and bottom-line thinking, studios long ago ceded artistic risk-taking to independent companies and talent.

What is new today is the vertical consolidation of different communication entities geared not only toward international marketplace imperatives but also to their own diverse internal needs. It is not only that company-owned studios need mass-market movies able to spin off into T-shirts, CDs, lunch boxes and toys that can be sold in company-owned stores. These conglomerates also own the means of distribution—television channels, cable and video companies, and, for the first time in 50 years, movie theaters themselves.

These company-owned outlets need product, preferably company-owned product. The conglomerates are snapping up successful independent companies to feed those needs, offering small companies a steady source of underwriting along with promises of creative noninterference. But what will happen if controversial film content challenges corporate images or threatens competing "family" interests? How long before corporate desire for full ownership and control of product turns these independent companies and filmmakers into company employees, beholden entirely to company will and policy? How will hitherto independent companies with diverse tastes like Castle Rock and New Line Pictures maintain their individuality when each is competing for material that will appeal to the same corporate parent? Finally, how will the genuinely independent filmmakers fund and distribute their risky work when a few monolithic corporations gain increasing control of the means of access to the public?

If any of these scenarios comes to pass, the recent mergers, building on already existing trends, will further constrain the ability of filmmakers to create, produce and distribute inventive and challenging movies. And that will be a loss, whether you are committed to creating films with a unique artistic vision or to experiencing their magic in the warm dark of a welcoming theater.

Barbara Maltby is an independent producer whose credits include A River Runs Through It, King of the Hill *and* The American President.

16

Off the Air

Lou Adler

When I told my wife of 36 years that I was writing an article on the subject of radio news, she said: "What radio news?" She has always had the facility to cut to the quick.

From where I sit, the future of radio news looks pretty grim. It's been in trouble for a long time, plagued by a combination of federal deregulation, market forces and mergers. And, ironically, the people who put radio news in trouble are not just businesspeople who might profit from no-news radio, but also the very journalists who stand to lose out in the new order of broadcasting.

For years, the National Association of Broadcasters fought to get government off the backs of the station owners who held their operating licenses under strict rules administered by the Federal Communications Commission. In essence, the FCC compelled owners to operate their stations in the public interest.

For the owners, deregulation made sense: Regulations restricted a licensee's freedom to make money. For example, one rule said that a certain percentage of any broadcast day must be devoted to news and public affairs programming. And news wasn't exactly a hot sale compared to entertainment.

The percentage requirement was a virtual "jobs for journalists" rule. But journalists, individually and through their own professional organizations, such as the Radio and Television News Directors Association, joined the fight for deregulation. Their complaint was "content" regulation. They said they could be fair without the FCC's "Fairness Doctrine," which demanded that stations deal with issues of public importance in a fair and balanced fashion.

When deregulation came, both the Fairness Doctrine and the concept of broadcasting as a public service were swept away. Any gains for radio news were overshadowed by regulatory changes on the business side, which set off developments that eventually undermined radio newsrooms.

One of the most important rules done away with was the "three year" regulation, which said that anyone acquiring a license had to hold it and operate the station for at least three years. It was a significant deterrent to heavy activity in license trading.

When the three-year rule was lifted, the station-trading frenzy of the 1980s followed. The floodgates were opened to the sharp-pencil crowd—those with no regard for broadcasting but a good sense for money-making. And money was in the quick trade: Buy low, improve the cash flow (cut overhead, eliminate the news department, automate) and then sell to the next guy. The banks, joint ventures and other financial sources reveled in it. Cash was plentiful—and cash was what it was all about.

At the same time, FM surged at the expense of AM. With a much purer and clearer signal, and in stereo to boot, FM was where the music was. And music was what the youth of America wanted to hear. (The older audience, except for those who spent a lot of time in their cars, was glued to the tube.) FM listening surpassed AM, bringing more staff cutbacks. Where to cut? The newsroom, of course.

Any hope of halting the decline of news on radio was put to rest by the Telecommunications Act of 1996. Radio regulation, which in my view was the only thing that made broadcasters truly responsible to the public, has disappeared. Practically all restraints on licenses have been lifted. The threat of license challenges, which was at least one incentive for responsible station operation, is effectively gone. And license terms, which were once three years, are now eight.

The Telecommunications Act does away with limits on the number of stations that can be controlled nationwide by one entity. It eases local radio ownership restrictions. And, as big broadcasters urged, it means more mergers.

With more mergers not only possible but probable, look for further retrenchment and a continuing diminution of radio news generally. In large markets, where the all-news format remains commercially viable, radio news will continue to be available around the clock. In smaller markets, radio news is likely to continue to shrink as more and more stations are gobbled up by groups with a tendency to reduce costs by programming all of their stations from one central location (with consequently smaller news staffs).

Meanwhile, consolidation continues. In New York City, for example, where WCBS-AM and WINS-AM were once fierce competitors, both are now owned by Westinghouse.

WCBS and WINS competed intensely for almost 30 years. I ran the WCBS newsroom for 10 of those years. I know how much that sense of competition meant to us all, how much it spurred us on to do our best to fight the good fight. Will the fact that both stations now march to the same tune, under the same battle flag, have a negative effect on journalistic incentives?

How would WCBS Radio have covered a story involving Westinghouse before the merger? How would it cover the story now? Does that scare you the way it scares me?

_____

Lou Adler, associate professor in the School of Mass Communications and director of the Ed McMahon Communications Center at Quinnipiac College, was operations and news director for WCBS and vice president of news for WOR. He is president of Eagle Media Productions Ltd., a radio program production and syndication company.

17

Conglomerates—A Good Thing for Books

Jonathan Karp

It was an otherwise upbeat lunch at one of those $12 hamburger palaces. The Company encourages colleagues from Sales and Editorial to network and brainstorm, so I was telling Steve about some of the authors I was editing and he was telling me about the lengths to which he was willing to go to get a book noticed, even it if meant traveling to a bookstore to set up an elaborate window display. We were getting along fine, when he said something that has haunted me to this day: "You know," he confessed, "I'd be perfectly happy if we didn't publish any new novels for a year or two. Our books would sell a lot better if there were a moratorium on fiction."

This seemed like a heretical and threatening idea. After all, aren't publishers supposed to produce new fiction? It might be more economical to reprint the classics year after year, but there certainly ought to be a place in our culture, and in our bookstores, for new voices and new stories. I knew Steve wasn't completely serious, but his logic was undeniable. In 1994, there were 5,415 novels published, according to *Publishers Weekly*. How many of them did *you* read?

Spurred by this conversation, I asked 15 of my colleagues at an editorial gathering whether they thought there was any real demand for the novels they are publishing. My question was met with silence, followed, rather lamely, by a consensus that it's a publisher's job to create the demand.

This explains the necessity of mergers in publishing. We are creating a product for which no great demand exists. We seek some influence over the process by which books are bought, but leisure products—whether novels or movie tickets or subscriptions to on-line services—are purchased on whims, incalculable desires.

If you work in publishing, you are working in a business that requires you to tame the tigers of caprice. In addition to the 5,415 novels published last year, we unloaded 46,448 nonfiction titles on an overwhelmed, distracted and enervated public. Every day, we try to devise clever ways of ramming a particular book through the barricades of bunk cluttering the public consciousness. There probably isn't a publisher alive today who wouldn't sleep with Oprah in exchange for an hour's worth of nationally televised book plugging. (Larry King is another matter entirely.)

The reason mergers make sense is, of course, control. Fewer media companies mean more control of inventory, greater distribution share and an amplified sales message—essential tools in storming the barricades. Writing in *Civilization*, veteran editor Richard Todd laments the disappearance of a shared reading culture. "It isn't books or talent that are dying, or even the literary sensibility, but a sense of literary community," he writes. "The world of readers has become an atomized world." With over 50,000 new titles every year, is it any wonder that people don't find themselves debating the merits of a particular book? It's a small miracle when two people on the same train are reading the same thing.

This may be overly idealistic, but if media companies continue to merge, perhaps they will gain the discipline to restrain their subsidiaries from publishing so much and force them to focus on those few books around which the mythical Common Reader can commune and discuss. We are capable of recreating a culture in which people can discuss books as passionately as they debate movies or share music, but to accomplish that publishers must exercise better control of distribution.

Media companies are no longer competing with one another. The competition is the Stairmaster, the family dinner or anything else that cuts into those few fixed hours of daily leisure time when books, newspapers or magazines might get read. Solitary and disenfranchised writers may not automatically regard big companies as their salvation, but in the midst of ever-increasing leisure opportunities, those companies devoted to written expression must be bigger and stronger to make their message heard.

Conglomerates are a good idea. Oligopolies would be even better.

Jonathan Karp is a senior editor at Random House.

18

Are Your Intentions Honorable?

Jerry Michalski

As media giants test the waters of new media, the key thing to watch is their intent. This may sound slightly loony, hard to do or unimportant, but it's actually the best way to understand where specific media companies are headed. These companies' current frenzy to ally, joint-venture, acquire or just announce *something* is partly a desperate gamble to gain market share, partly an effort to reconfigure companies so they end up owning high-margin slices of the future food chain. Few major media companies will survive this period with their market shares intact. What distinguishes companies with viable strategies from those without is their intent.

To explain the role of intent, we must first explain what is new about new media. It's *not* the opportunity to spend a lot of money to digitize movies and other media, squish them so they fit through all-new pipes and cables, then play them at nearly the same quality that the traditional analog technology delivers. It *may* be this mysterious thing called "interactivity." But if you ask three people what interactivity is, you're likely to get six answers—none of them particularly helpful.

What *is* new is that ordinary people and ordinary companies now have inexpensive access to a new platform for communications—the Internet. Until now, there were only two topologies for electronic communication: point-to-point (phone calls and faxes) and broadcast (practically everything else, including physical goods such as books, magazines, newspapers, music and movies). Anyone can use the phone

123

system, but it has limited functionality. In general, the phone system connects two people at a time. When they are done talking, there is no artifact left behind, beyond a phone bill. People generally know whom they call before they place the call—they don't browse the phone system.

The other topology—broadcasting—is the province of the major media companies. They own it completely. Ordinary people and companies have extremely limited access to it. There is no feedback loop that matters. Public-access cable TV is generally a joke; letters to the editor appear many issues after the offending article. Media producers can and do treat their audiences as "consumers": people whom they want to train to consume. Advertising plays a crucial role in these businesses' revenue models. Often the content is merely a vehicle for the ads.

Now, with the astonishingly swift growth of on-line services and Internet connectivity, many new topologies for communication are emerging. That is, people can now easily communicate with each other (and a few dozen acquaintances) over e-mail, or with much larger communities of interest on electronic bulletin boards, Internet news groups and mailing lists. They can publish materials for others to bump into on the World Wide Web, or build imaginary spaces with fantastic furniture and demonic devices inside of multiuser game environments. People can type to each other at the same time (a surprisingly compelling pastime that's quite profitable for the service providers), or add live audio and video feeds. Today, all of these features have odd names and require some technical knowledge to set up and run, but they are quickly being woven together into a new fabric for electronic communications and publishing that is accessible to all.

The magic of these new places and spaces is that they allow people to find and meet each other, to leave things behind for others to stumble upon and perhaps use. A teen-age boy puts movie reviews on the Web, and thousands of people drop by to read them. A professor at the University of Singapore publishes a list of resources about electronic commerce, and hundreds of people interested in the subject access it as a valuable source of links to information. A woman who travels a lot puts her calendar on the Web, and tens of friends and relatives check it periodically to see when she will be near them. None of these items is expensive to put and keep on line.

In fact, people can build Web sites using the same PCs and Internet connections that they need now to do their jobs. They don't really need advertisements, although extra cash helps as sites get larger, or as site owners decide to turn their avocations into vocations. Smart companies will sponsor sites that are relevant to their products or communities. Small, personal, organic sites will flourish by the thousands. The sites that will suffer are those from media giants, most of whom have spent too much on the medium as they battle each other for "eyeballs."

The new medium isn't about eyeballs, however. It's about relationships. The appropriate approach is sociology, not behavioral psychology (particularly the behavioral conditioning that ad agencies have mastered). Not that the Internet renders Skinner, Maslow and Pavlov's theories inoperative overnight. It's just that now there is more access, balance and flexibility. The feedback loops have closed. One small group of companies no longer owns and controls the medium, and it is highly unlikely—though not impossible—that they might step in and dominate the new one. The most promising evidence that they won't dominate it is their continued inability to understand the medium and create sustainable business models.

If we can all publish to each other, will we continue to look at things created by the media giants? Yes, clearly. Media will not disappear. Movies won't suddenly become interactive, with audiences jointly determining the outcomes. Narrative is essential. Storytelling is one of the oldest skills. Media companies will no longer own the whole market, but their products will still be valued.

More importantly, editorial judgment matters, and media conglomerates have hired plenty of it. The communities that are creating and recreating resource lists and discussions about every topic imaginable need help sorting what matters from what doesn't and presenting it all in compelling, accessible ways. These communities are creating the context within which other pieces must live. The editor's role in this setting isn't to stay separate from the audience, but rather to engage the audience actively. This kind of editorial judgment isn't applied from afar; it is transmitted up close. Sometimes their efforts are compelling; other times they could use support and training.

A few media companies will see this as an opportunity and change their roles and relationships. They will begin to think of themselves as communications companies and figure out ways to engage their customers on their customers' terms. They will join forces with many of the same companies with which they might have wanted to work earlier, but with different intent.

Think of this as part of a larger movement to reintegrate society, to close the gap between ordinary people (the passive "consumers") and so-called experts. The Net helps us take more responsibility for our actions, words and selves. It brings expertise (and the experts themselves) to our doorstep. Publishers and telecommunications companies may well merge, but what they do with their merged talents will be very different from the dystopian, one-way, video-on-demand future that seems to have motivated such mergers before.

Jerry Michalski is managing editor of Release 1.0, *a monthly newsletter about the future of communication and computing technology. He can be reached at spiff@edventure.com or www.edventure.com.*

VI

The Consequences of Media Empires Around the World

19

A Very Hard Market

Stephen Vines

It has taken a little while to sink in, but it is now becoming very apparent to global media conglomerates that selling their services in the booming Asian market is not quite the same as selling Coke or Pepsi to this increasingly affluent and product-hungry group of consumers.

There is no question that the Asian market, specifically the East Asian market, is the place to be for international companies eager to expand sales. However, some of the biggest players in the media business have appeared to underestimate just how difficult it is to operate in this region where governments are notably wary of foreign media influence. While some of the world's biggest media companies, including Dow Jones, NBC and CNN from the United States; the BBC, the Pearson Group and Hachette from Europe; as well as News Corp. from Australia, remain committed to establishing a presence here in Asia, they have pitifully small profits to show for their commitment.

The Dow Jones Corp. was one of the pioneers in Asia, where it has invested in Asian news wire services, newspapers, magazines and a television station. It has spent two decades establishing a place in the market for an Asian edition of the *Wall Street Journal* and has succeeded in producing a strong editorial product but still struggles to achieve an Asia-wide circulation exceeding 50,000 copies. An investment in the relatively new Asia Business Network (ABN), a business-oriented television station distributed throughout the region by satellite and cable, has yet to yield profits, and some Hong Kong-based analysts are skeptical about whether it will in the near future.

Arguably the most successful of Dow Jones' investments is the *Far East Economic Review*, based in Hong Kong. This magazine was founded in the British colony and is not perceived as an "American product"; indeed, its strength lies in its local knowledge and longtime editorial presence in the markets it seeks to serve. Nevertheless, Dow Jones has had a rough ride in East Asia, where it focuses its marketing efforts. Both the Asian *Wall Street Journal* and the *Far East Economic Review* have suffered distribution bans, notably in Singapore, where sales are still restricted. ABN, although based in Singapore, is still denied distribution in the island state.

Other major media corporations have also faced the wrath of local governments. Rupert Murdoch's Star TV satellite television network incurred the extreme displeasure of the Chinese government by carrying BBC World Service Television, which, among other "crimes," broadcast a program about the late Zhisui Li's best-selling biography of Chairman Mao Tse-tung. Murdoch added fuel to the fire by (accurately) describing the international electronic media as a threat to authoritarian regimes. Star TV's hopes for making a major impact on the Chinese market were rapidly put to rest, the BBC was hurriedly withdrawn from Star broadcasts aimed at China, and News Corp. has spent most of the last couple of years vigorously kowtowing to the rulers in Beijing.

China, like other authoritarian powers, simply does not understand, let alone tolerate, the concept of free media. At a conference held in Beijing in February, Zeng Jianhui, director of the Information Office of the State Council, and therefore one of the nation's most senior media controllers, explained how he saw the role of media. "The fundamental interests of the country must be resolutely defended in the [media] work," he said, "and principles must be adhered to strictly in matters concerning state sovereignty, national interests and national prestige."

Zeng was merely reiterating a well-established policy of insisting that the media serve state interests, a view that tends not to be accepted by the Western media, including aspirants to a presence in Asia. Whereas the domestic media can be made to accept this policy, there are no guarantees of the same level of cooperation from the international media coming into this country.

One of the most articulate critics of the overseas media's efforts to establish a presence in Asia is Malaysia's Prime Minister Mahathir Mohamad. He argues that the Western media has a set of alien values that it wishes to impose on Asians and fears that "gullible" Asians may be unduly influenced by international media organizations. Referring, for example, to attempts by News Corp. to gain a foothold in Malaysia through its Sky TV network, Dr. Mahathir told a British audience last year, "We will not allow Rupert Murdoch to decide for us what we should do," adding in typically robust style, "if Murdoch does not like it he can go and boil himself." He went further, saying that the media in some Western societies had run out of control. "The people and their leaders live in fear," he said, "fear of the free media which they so loudly proclaim as inviolable."

China, Malaysia and Singapore are not alone in resisting the intervention of foreign media organizations, with the significant exception of news agencies, although even China, for example, is trying to ensure that it gets a cut (over and above taxation) of all news-agency business done within its borders. In Asia, state resistance to the presence of overseas media organization is the norm. In India, for example, there has been much talk of relaxing rules barring any foreign ownership of domestic newspapers, a source of great frustration to the British Pearson group, which established a joint venture with its flagship *Financial Times* newspaper, but the deal remains stillborn despite all editorial arrangements having been put in place some time ago. In Indonesia controls on the media are getting tighter, and any form of foreign presence is barely tolerated.

Perhaps surprisingly, a more relaxed attitude has been shown by Vietnam's communist government, which has allowed foreign companies to enter into joint ventures with state media, albeit under tight control. Both Australian and Singaporean companies have taken advantage of this relaxation although the going has not been easy. More predictably, countries such as Thailand and the Philippines are more hospitable to foreign investors (although the latter less so), reflecting their generally more democratic systems of government.

Hong Kong, a British colony, has become the region's *de facto* media center, owing to the absence of state controls and a *laissez-faire* attitude toward the media. Thus foreign interests have stakes in local television stations and newspapers and use the colony as a base for regional publication and broadcasting. NBC has established an Asian satellite network operating out of Hong Kong, CNN uses the territory as the regional distribution center and a whole host of regional publications is based here.

However, a long shadow looms over the media in Hong Kong, which will revert to Chinese sovereignty next year and will almost certainly come under tighter control, despite promises that the territory will be allowed to maintain its way of life after the change of power. Day by day, Chinese officials demonstrate their inability to appreciate how a free media operates and signal every intention to impose controls.

Last August representatives from the Hong Kong Newspaper Society, a publishers association, traveled to Beijing to seek assurances of continued press freedom. These were duly delivered but immediately qualified by the Vice-Premier Qian Qichen, who has been given overall responsibility for Hong Kong affairs. Qian said that he wanted the media to observe three guidelines: first, to promote a "loving China and Hong Kong spirit"; second, to confine news reporting to a basis of "fact"; and third, to handle news in an ethical and responsible way.

What does that really mean? The answer was unwittingly supplied five months earlier by Wu Gaofu, the director of the Taiwan, Hong Kong and Macau News Research Center, based at the University of Wuhan in central China. "There must be some form of control over the Hong Kong media" after 1997, he said. "It is impossible for there not to be, just like here in China, where we have both central and local control over every locality." He added, "We must talk about what truth means in journalism, and morality in the media." Maybe that means that the controls will only apply to the domestic media, but that view is looking increasingly improbable. Last May the Hong Kong-based but Beijing-controlled *Ta Kung Pao* newspaper, which is often used to float the views of the Chinese leadership preceding formal announcements, said in an editorial that the presence of international media organizations in Hong Kong would need to be re-examined after 1997. "Since some of these organizations are official or semi-official . . . China must study and decide on their presence in Hong Kong after July 1, 1997," said the editorial.

Media organizations based in Taiwan are clearly a target. But these strictures may also apply, for example, to the BBC, Agence France-Presse, Voice of America and other organizations that are wholly or partly owned and controlled by overseas governments. It is no exaggeration to state that every international media organization using Hong Kong as a regional base is making tentative plans for a move should this be necessary after 1997. The real problem is where to go, because the alternatives are not obvious. Countries like Thailand and the Philippines, which are politically hospitable, suffer from serious infrastructure shortcomings. Countries such as Singapore and Malaysia, with good infrastructure, suffer from the imposition of potentially unacceptable controls. Some thought is being given to moving to Sydney, Australia, but its geographic remoteness is problematic. The situation is very similar to that facing media organizations upon the outbreak of the Lebanese civil war in 1979, when Beirut ceased to be an acceptable regional base. Some companies moved to Cyprus, others to Jordan or farther afield to London and Paris. But none of these locations was able to serve as a satisfactory Middle East media center.

If the region is becoming increasingly inhospitable to foreign media multinationals, it may just be that conditions are better for Asian companies seeking to establish a regional presence. Since the mid to late 1980s, there has been a noticeable increase in cross-regional expansion by Asian-owned media companies that feel they are outgrowing their limited domestic markets. Among the first to think in regional terms was the cash-rich Singapore Press Holdings group, which initially planned to make one of its papers, *Business Times*, into a regional publication. However, SPH is a very conservative company that tends to move at a snail's pace. The *Business Times* plan was aborted, but SPH cautiously proceeded to buy stakes in Hong Kong's leading English-language daily, the *South China Morning Post*, and in a new Thai business daily.

Meanwhile the *South China Morning Post* fell under the wing of an unlikely new media mogul, Malaysian businessman Robert Kuok, better known for his property, sugar and hotel interests. He bought out Murdoch's controlling stake in the *Post* and took a larger stake in Television Broadcast Ltd. (TVB), Hong Kong's leading television station. TVB is controlled by Sir Run Run Shaw, best known as a maker of *kung fu* films.

Sir Run Run, meanwhile, has been trying to leverage his dominant position in the Hong Kong television market by creating a satellite television station broadcasting to Chinese-speaking communities in Asia. Another Hong Kong entrepreneur, the controversial C.P. Yu, has poured vast sums of money into a CNN-style Chinese cable news network. Both ventures are doing badly, but they are still in their early days.

Perhaps the most ambitious regional media baron is the Thai entrepreneur Sondhi Limthongkul (I am a consulting editor for one of his papers) whose M Group is involved in all aspects of the media. He makes no bones about his intention to become the head of Asia's most influential media conglomerate. He has launched an Asian regional business daily, a regional glossy business magazine, an on-line information service and a clutch of regional trade publications, a regional conference organization and, in cooperation with the Lao government, is launching a satellite for television broadcasts.

Sondhi believes that the future of the region lies with people like himself, not outsiders such as CNN's Ted Turner and News Corp.'s Murdoch. As he sees it, they do not appreciate regional sensitivities or ways of doing things. He aggressively promotes an "Asia for Asians" philosophy, which is striking a chord, particularly among the urban middle class who are most likely to be consumers of regional media products. Sondhi's critics say he is overreaching himself by talking big and delivering small.

It remains to be seen who is right. As matters stand, neither the Western-based media multinational nor Asian-based media companies are making any real money out of regional services in Asia. This is a very hard market, and it may be impossible to crack.

Stephen Vines, founding editor of the Hong Kong newspaper Eastern Express, *writes about East Asia for the* British Independent. *He consults on media matters for the* Asia Times *of Bangkok and a number of other companies.*

20

Foreign Capital Is Welcome Here

Mihály Gálik

Once upon a time . . . One feels tempted to begin an essay on the transformation of the media in Central and Eastern Europe this way, even though it started only a few years ago. The old command press of communism looks so strange right now, like part of a tired ghost story, because the media landscape of Central and Eastern Europe is being remade. And a significant part of its transformation is due to the arrival of international media conglomerates from Western Europe and the United States.

For half a century after World War II, Central and Eastern European media systems were frozen in a certain political, institutional, economic and legal structure that was broken during the revolutionary changes of 1989–90. The legal and institutional structure that governed the media in Hungary was typical of that found in other communist countries. All newspapers and periodicals and all radio and television programs were controlled directly or indirectly by the ruling Hungarian Socialist Workers' Party. Although freedom of the press was guaranteed in the constitution, and a separate press law was passed by Parliament in 1986 (at the very end of the regime), the law was a mere facade. The infamous Hungarian press law of 1986 not only denied citizens the right to found any publishing organization but also required them to obtain a license from existing state- or party-owned publishing houses to publish new titles. The license was formally granted or denied by a state authority. The informal control exercised by the ruling party and the formal state control over entering the industry were accompanied by carefully designed directives related to the day-to-day operations of publishing houses: All strategic decisions were made by party or state authorities.

The collapse of the ruling party's dominance over the media was a clear sign of the decline of the old regime. In autumn of 1988 in Hungary, a few independent weeklies and fortnightlies were licensed as a political concession to the opposition forces. In June of 1989, the licensing system was abolished, and this event, together with the provisions of the Act on Business Associations enacted six months earlier, cleared the way for foreign investors to enter the media industries.

Magazine publishing was an especially appealing target. State and party authorities did not believe that consumer magazines were essential reading for citizens, so there were few such titles on the market. Unsatisfied demand on a large scale, supported by a booming advertising market and then-low newsprint prices, made room for rapid market expansion. New magazines devoted to fashion, sex, television programs, automobiles, women's issues, the home, youth and hobbies appeared on the market in short order.

Hungary's economy, like the other command economies of the region, suffered from a built-in shortage of capital. Consequently, investments required to publish these new titles were financed mostly by foreign investors. They knew how real media markets function and almost took it for granted that the same features would prevail in Hungary. They were right. Multinational companies, like Axel Springer of Germany and Bonnier from Sweden, entered the market. Smaller firms, mainly German and American, also founded or bought publishing houses and tried to get a share in the Hungarian market.

For the press, the most dramatic institutional changes occurred in the daily newspaper industry. The large old publishing houses that had been dominant for decades could not defend themselves against market forces. Due to the chaos created by the collapse of the old regime, they practically lost the titles they had published earlier. Foreign investors—multinational media empires like Bertelsmann and Axel Springer, Rupert Murdoch's News Corp., Robert Maxwell's Mirror Group, Robert Hersant's Socpresse from France and some smaller Austrian groups as well—took over. Taking advantage of the loopholes built into legal regulation left over from the old regime, these groups transferred into private ownership most of the national dailies and all but one regional daily in just a couple of months during 1990.

In many cases, Hungarian journalists supported these efforts. While journalists had played an important role in hastening the change from "goulash communism" to democracy, as elections approached the opposition parties made public statements about purges at state-owned publishers. Journalists who worked in such enterprises felt little choice but to support foreign companies in taking over.

Yet the role of media multinationals in Hungary must be understood in its proper context. By their own standards the new arrivals didn't invest too much capital, just a couple of million dollars. It was only in 1995 that Hebdo International from Canada paid about $20 million for the right to publish a Hungarian daily composed of classified advertisements, *Express*, the most profitable title on the market and the flagship of the only surviving state-owned publishing house. And these sums look like peanuts if you consider the privatization of telecoms in the region: Deutsche Telecom and Ameritech, for example, paid nearly $2 billion to buy a two-thirds share in MATAV, the Hungarian telephone company. They planned to invest the same amount of money from 1994 to 1997. However, foreign investments in publishing, while relatively small, do hasten the transition from a command economy to a market economy.

The foreign investors typically promised in writing to fulfill certain conditions for editorial staff members, who felt threatened by the emerging political regime and calls for purges at state publishers. Standard concerns included computerization of editorial processes, investment in printing, job security for one or two years, editorial and political independence, and higher salaries. Looking back, these promises by and large were kept.

Of course, the entry of foreign capital was not limited to the privatization of existing firms or titles. Foreign investors, working mainly in joint ventures with Hungarian capital, launched tabloid and middlebrow newspapers—the kind that were in short supply. Not surprisingly, the share of these two submarkets is growing continuously at the expense of "quality" national dailies. Publishing a quality daily costs a lot of money, and the Hungarian market does not support this. People are not willing to pay much more for a quality daily, and publishers are not willing to invest too much to improve quality enough to ultimately convince readers that their newspaper is worth the high price. The market is small, readership is rather general, and, at least in the short run, advertising revenues could not balance the increased costs. It is a vicious circle that is very hard to break out of—not only in Hungary but throughout Central and Eastern Europe.

In Hungary the share of foreign ownership in the press is extremely high. (In the rest of Central and Eastern Europe this share is not as high but still significant.) The two submarkets, national and regional/ local dailies, show a slightly different picture. In 1996, among national dailies, 60 percent of the total daily newspaper market belongs to companies with a foreign majority interest.

Among regional (county) dailies, some 75 percent of the total daily newspaper market belongs to companies with a foreign majority interest. The comparable market share in Poland and the Czech Republic is about 50 percent. (The main difference between the two countries is that in the Polish national market foreign publishers have a weak position.) Otherwise, newspaper market concentration is not higher than elsewhere in Western Europe.

The dynamics of the national dailies' market in Hungary are characterized in the preceding graph. After Robert Maxwell's death in 1992, the Mirror Group's interest was bought by a Swiss publisher, Jurg Marquard of Ost Presse. Murdoch's News Corp. pulled out in the same year; Hersant's Socpresse in the next one. Their interests were sold to companies with a state majority, and the titles in question got privatized again only in 1995. (The commercial bank that bought these titles is partly owned by Austrian investors, but they do not have majority interest.) The Swiss Ringier and the American Gannett publishers launched *Blikk*, the first Hungarian color tabloid, in 1994 as a joint venture.

The magazine market in Hungary is highly concentrated and more segmented than the newspaper market. The share of the largest publisher, Axel Springer-Budapest Ltd., might amount to one-third of total sales turnover. German magazine publishers play a very active role in other Central and Eastern European countries, too, but the level of concentration there is less than in Hungary. Everywhere, the boom of the early '90s is over, competition is very strong and, in many cases, titles and their publishers fight for survival.

Foreign newspaper publishers who ventured into Central and Eastern Europe, with their firsthand experience in the relative stability and profitability of markets, invested first in printing and later in distribution. They built up vertical integration and followed the trends of

FIGURE 20.1
Share of Publishing Houses with a Foreign Majority Interest
on the Market of National Dailies in Hungary, 1991–96

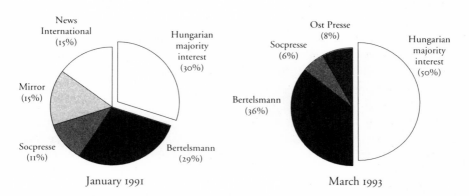

source: Juhász, G. "Changes on the Press Market, 1990–1993," *Political Yearbook of Hungary, 1994*. Budapest: The Center for Hungarian Democracy Studies Foundation.

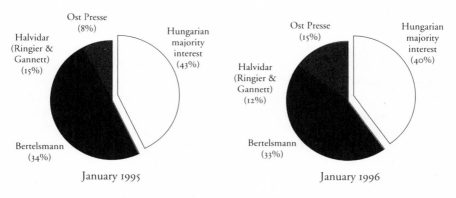

source: Data gathered by G. Juhász and M. Gálik.

mature newspaper markets. Compared to the bargain prices they paid for taking over the titles that had been on the market earlier, they had to invest a lot of money to modernize the newspaper industry. There were also serious investments in privatized printing plants for producing high-quality consumer magazines.

In broadcasting, the transition from communist control to the new era of international media conglomerates is another story. The new regimes in Central and Eastern Europe have been far from eager to give up their control of radio and television. Allowing private radio and television has not been a question of utmost urgency in the region, and the reason behind it seems quite clear: Governments fear losing influence over society's most influential media. Hungary has just passed a broadcasting bill, and two national terrestrial television channels are to be auctioned in late 1996. In the absence of the bill only a couple dozen local and regional broadcasters could get licenses, so their market share is still marginal.

While the American presence in Hungarian broadcasting is more pronounced than the American influence in print media, the strength of state broadcasting has tended to limit the influence of American firms. Nevertheless, the largest regional radio broadcaster has been under American control since 1994. And the largest investment in the Hungarian private sector went into cable when United Holding International Co., a joint venture of Time Warner, US West and TCI, spent $30 million during the '90s via its subsidiary, Kabelkom Ltd., on the distribution of HBO cable television programs in Hungary.

The Hungarian broadcasting bill itself has a 49 percent upper limit of interest to any individual or business group in terrestrial television broadcasting on the national market. It requires that at least 26 percent of the shares be owned by Hungarian citizens or business groups registered in the country, and the majority of board members must have Hungarian citizenship and permanent residency in the country. In spite of these limitations, it appears certain that foreign investors will play the lead in this field as well. Some $100 million will be needed to pay for these two licenses and to cover the losses of the first years in business. Leaving aside the financial risk involved, this is too much capital to raise in Hungary alone. Due to the strict rules against cross-ownership built into the bill, the multinational media conglomerates already present in the country have a small chance to expand their activities and dominate national broadcasting markets. Nevertheless, investors will surely appear.

The Czech Republic, however, provides an example of relevant and profitable privatization in television broadcasting. Nova Television, the private Czech broadcaster with American majority interest—cosmetics giant Estee Lauder Co.'s money can be found in the background—enjoys a monopoly status in the commercial sphere and has become a market leader, getting about 70 percent of the audience. Nova has capitalized on its singular position under the law and has been able to make money from the very beginning. This is good news for the shareholders of Nova Television, but the peculiarity of Czechs dismantling a state television monopoly only to create one in the private sector has confounded neutral observers. A private monopoly in commercial television broadcasting is hardly a situation that fits with democracy and a market economy. In Poland, by contrast, even though a broadcasting bill was passed years ago, a legal stalemate has allowed the state broadcaster to keep its *de facto* monopoly in television.

We are all aware nowadays that the transition out of communism is a long and controversial process. In 1989–90 everything seemed possible. Right now the limits to change are more evident. Waiting for years to privatize broadcasting has done a lot of political harm and wasted resources throughout Central and Eastern Europe. And the successful Czech case has so many side effects that you can raise the question of whose success it is anyway.

Central and Eastern Europeans can't just jump into the realm of ideal democratic media. They also have to reconcile themselves with the less shiny parts of the media market, including relations with international media conglomerates. Looking back, it is apparent that there was a special trade-off between the share of foreign ownership and the privatization of the press in 1989–90: If foreign conglomerates and foreign capital had not entered Hungary and other countries in the region, we might still be living with state-run press systems.

Mihály Gálik is an associate professor at the Budapest University of Economic Sciences and a research fellow at the European Institute for the Media in Düsseldorf, Germany.

21

In the Company of Giants

Mac Margolis

Not many years ago, in a town in the Amazon region of Brazil, I watched an enterprising hot dog vendor mount a black-and-white television on his trailer, which was parked strategically at the edge of a public plaza. In a studied ritual, he fit the 12–inch screen with a tinted filter, giving the images the illusion of color. He set out folding metal chairs, and one by one the townspeople took their places. Friends and neighbors and strangers communed under a moonless sky, dispatching hot dogs and beer as the nightly episode of the latest televised *novella*, or soap opera, flickered dreamily across the dusty screen.

It's hard to imagine such a drowsy scenario in our highly wired times, now that Latin Americans everywhere can tune into the wide world at the touch of a remote. But just a couple of generations ago, they were innocents—especially in Brazil, a nation that is both centerpiece and symbol of the great changes now taking place in the media systems of Latin America.

In the Brazil of 1950, a nation of 50 million, there were only about 2,000 clunky black-and-white television consoles. Twenty years later, when Brazil was on its way to winning a third soccer World Cup, the whole staff of TV Globo, the leading national network, piled into the director's office to cheer their team as it appeared on a color television, one of three in all of Rio de Janeiro.

Today, if you scour the backlands of the drought-parched northeast or the bogs of the Pantanal marshlands, you might still find an entrepreneur with a trailer and TV, working a makeshift amphitheater at *telenovella* time. But there is another Brazil on the air today. This one has no less than 36 million homes with television and a potential audience of 120 million. Forests of parabolic antennae sprout from the hillsides of farm country and atop the glass and steel skyline of Sâo Paulo. Coaxial and fiber-optic cable burrow under the urban asphalt. Pay television, barely five years old, is already booming, and interactive TV is within sight. Corporate investors the world over have ventured into Brazil, claiming their stake in one of the most promising television markets on the planet. Brazilians are now swimming in channels and programs.

The makers of local television have also come a long way. Until well into the 1980s, Brazilian broadcasting was a closed and intimate shop. As in the rest of Latin America, television was the domain of a few vastly powerful family dynasties who enjoyed sure profits and captive audiences. To be sure, many of these Latin dynasties—the Cisneroses of Venezuela, the Azcárragas of Mexico and the Marinhos of Brazil—managed to professionalize their operations. But thanks to a long tradition of laws barring foreigners from national television, and the special, often cozy relations these media titans cultivated with the ruling regimes, the competition at home was always timid.

But by the middle of this decade, the comfortable world of Latin American network television had been turned on its head, and nowhere more so than in Brazil. By the end of 1995, two media empires, Rede Globo de Televisâo (TV Globo) and Editora Abril, the biggest publishing house, had sealed bold joint ventures with the most powerful communications conglomerates on the planet. In early 1995, Editora Abril joined forces with two companies from the United States, Capital Cities/ABC and Hughes Communications, and two more from Latin America, Joaquín Vargas' MVS Multivisión of Mexico and Gustavo Cisneros' Venevisión of Venezuela. Globo followed suit and threw in with Rupert Murdoch's Australian-based News Corp., Emilio Azcárraga's Televisa of Mexico and America's Tele-Communications Inc. (TCI), the largest cable TV company in the world. The rival groups announced plans to beam subscription television throughout Latin America and have committed to investing a total of $1 billion in the next few years.

These developments were more than new business ventures. Together, they represented a new mindset for Latin Americans. Gringo capital, long a cultural taboo and often barred outright by national constitutions, was suddenly being openly and eagerly courted from the Rio Grande to Patagonia. The rapid development of television technology, and the lure of great profits to be made there, ended the old habit of isolation in Latin America. Mexico, Venezuela and Argentina all had embraced subscription television in the 1980s. (The real prize, of course, is network television, with its vast audiences. But network systems are closed to foreigners.) By 2000, industry observers reckon that Latin America will have almost 18 million subscribers and will absorb $4 billion in investments.

Brazil got off to a late start, but the size of the market and its thirst for innovation made up for the initial hesitancy. Even before these foreign alliances began to inject their money and methods, Brazilian pay-TV was a business waiting to boom. Subscriptions grew steadily, from a handful in 1991 to 240,000 at the beginning of 1994. Today there are 1.3 million customers, and subscriptions are growing at a clip of 10 percent per month, making Brazil "the fastest growing market in the world," as Alberto Pecegueiro, general director of TV Globo's cable service, Net-Globosat, likes to boast. By the year 2001, industry officials reckon that customers will have jumped to 6 million. The menu of channels has soared, from half a dozen to 50. In another year, there will be four times that many.

Just what all this means for the world of Brazilian television is not yet clear. Who will come out on top in this scramble for Brazil's television viewers? Will the foreign media conglomerates, with their aggressive merge-and-grow tactics, overwhelm the longtime national dynasties? Will the local programming be eclipsed by the dizzying offer of foreign channels? And what to make of all this puzzling new technology and its alphabet soup of acronyms—MMDS, DTH, KU band and IntelSat? "It's like you took all the underdeveloped countries at once to a technology fair in Los Angeles," says Homero Icaza Sanchez, a longtime television critic who runs surveys for broadcasters. "Everybody wants the latest gadget." Perhaps the only certainty is that the once-placid world of national television will never be the same.

Brazilian businesses have long enjoyed official aid and comfort in making everything from canned goods to computers. Television was equally coddled. Backed by constitutional bans against outsiders, the central government controlled the domestic broadcast market and severely restricted the number of TV concessions. The few impresarios who got into television early had a vital edge, and held it. A booming consumer-goods industry put Brazilian-made televisions (no imports, thank you) in home after home, and an ambitious military regime wired the nation with a tangle of transmission towers from the southern pampas to the Amazon basin. Brazil was a bell jar economy with rabbit-ear antennae.

Roberto Marinho, the owner of the colossal TV Globo, did not invent these rules, but they suited him just fine. Though Marinho acquired his television concession before the military coup of 1964, his amiable relations with the men in uniform—he was a personal friend to all five ruling generals—served him well. Marinho, a consummate diplomat, bowed to the censors when he had to, stood his ground when he dared and watched his network prosper. Much of the credit for Globo's success is his alone. Already a successful publisher, Marinho launched his television network in 1965, when he was 60, an age when most men are thinking of retirement. Unlike his early rivals, he had the guts to reinvest his profits into Globo year after year, and the sense to keep family and corporate affairs separate by hiring professionals to run the day-to-day operations.

The work and wit paid off. In a decade, Globo reigned supreme. It is hard to underestimate his sway in this sprawling country. In few democracies is television as important as it is in Brazil. Nationwide, 21 percent of adults—and up to 50 percent in the poorest regions—are illiterate. Brazil's 323 newspapers enjoy a total circulation of around 8 million. Television, by contrast, can reach 120 million people, more than three quarters of Brazil's population of 155 million. The last census showed more households with televisions than refrigerators. In a country that reads little but where people may flock to a public plaza to watch a single TV set, television provides entertainment, information and a daily fantasy. This captive audience belonged, for the most part, to Roberto Marinho.

True, there were five other networks, but Globo traditionally sopped up as much as 70 percent of audience and, not coincidentally, 75 percent of advertising revenues. Though its share of both has dropped in the past decade due to competition, Marinho rarely looks over his shoulder. "Globo has first, second and third place, in television," says one of the competitors. "All the rest come in at a distant fourth." Citizen Marinho, they began to call him—a "*de facto* minister of culture," many politicians say, only half jokingly. "It's like the big angelfish in the bowl who comes along and eats up all the others," said one of Globo's founders.

So, with Brazil firmly in hand, why shake things up with new, risky partnerships and ambitious multimillion-dollar deals? Globo had already been burned once, when Marinho's eldest son, Roberto Irineu Marinho, lost $120 million on a failed foreign adventure, the Italian-based Telemontecarlo. In an interview in the late 1980s, Marinho dismissed the idea of direct satellite broadcast television to Brazil as "premature." There was, of course, the daunting myth of the day—that pay-TV was going to be the ruin of the world's networks. What is more, many politicians simply looked down their noses at pay-TV because it was not a medium that spoke to the *povão*—the masses— where the real treasure of votes lay. TV insiders suggest that Marinho might never have gotten involved in pay television had he not been pushed.

Despite the legal restrictions, parabolic antennae began to crop up all over Brazil, from ranchers' estates to *favelas*, the hillside slums. Transmissions from all over the world could now be pirated into Brazilian living rooms. "Marinho is a powerful man, but he couldn't go against the laws of physics. What was he going to do, go around covering the country under umbrellas?" comments Rubens Glasberg, the editor and publisher of *PayTV*, a trade magazine.

In the end, it was not fear of foreigners that moved Marinho, but rather competition on the home front. At the time, there were four other television networks. One of them, SBT, run by the popular gabber and variety show host Silvio Santos, was eating away at Globo's audience with hard-hitting newscasts and daring *telenovellas*. Yet the real challenge came from outside of television, from Roberto Civita, the patriarch of a $1.2 billion family-run publishing empire, Editora Abril. Abril had tried for years to win a broadcast channel, but word was that the Civitas were just too independent-minded for the military to trust them with a TV concession.

When civilian rule was restored in the late 1980s, Abril finally got its chance. Civita launched a single-channel, closed-circuit service. Not to be outdone, Globo unfurled its own version, an analog transmission system, beamed to large parabolic satellite dishes. Both companies took fabulous losses—Marinho buried around $65 million, and Abril perhaps twice that. But by the new decade, pay television was

FIGURE 21.1
Top Media Firms by Continent

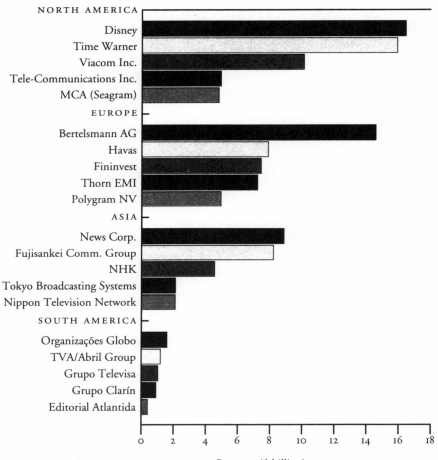

Revenue ($ billion)

SOURCES: *Television Business International: Yearbook '96; Variety: Special Collector's Edition Supplement* (Aug. 28–Sept. 3, 1995; *America Economia* (No. 105, March 1996); Audits & Surveys Worldwide; *Multichannel News International* (September 1995)

born. TV Abril (TVA) developed a wireless transmission (MMDS) system, upgrading to conventional cable where more subscriber density justified the expense.

Globo sent longtime network wizard Antonio Athayde to comb the globe for new methods and machinery. Athayde discovered that much of the television world had gone to cable. So Marinho set about to cable Brazil. TVA and Net-Globosat, the two "narrowcasters," are now running nearly neck and neck in a burgeoning market. Their 1.3 million subscriber base is expected to double by 1997.

Problems still abound. The investments in pay-TV are far fatter than the returns. Advertisers are "reticent," says Pecegueiro, the aggressive young head of Globosat. "Prudent" is the word that advertisers prefer. Last year, pay-TV rang up a mere $15 million in ad billings, a pittance when compared to the total $2.7 billion lavished on broadcast television. It is likely to take several years and millions more subscribers to win away some of the traditional network bounty to pay-TV. And the only source for the kind of money necessary to make that happen lay beyond national borders.

As it happened, the U.S.-based Hughes Communications Inc. was looking to expand into Latin America. After getting the cold shoulder from Marinho, in early 1995 Hughes announced a regional pact with junior partners in Brazil's TVA, Cisneros' Venevisión and Vargas' MVS Multivisión. They called the joint venture Galaxy Latin America and proclaimed some $500 million in investments for the coming years.

Back in Brazil, Civita conjured his own enterprise for satellite television, raising another $150 million and recruiting partners in Falcon Cable, Hearst Television and Capital Cities/ABC, recently acquired by Disney. Last July, wearing a Mickey Mouse T-shirt, Civita announced the new marriage and plans to launch a satellite television project, to transmit dozens of channels directly to homes fitted with pizza-sized parabolic antennae by way of the powerful KU satellite band.

Never one to be upstaged, Globo struck its own satellite deal last September, with Rupert Murdoch's News Corp., Televisa of Mexico and America's TCI. The new venture has no name as yet, but this "gang of four" (as the competition mischievously dubbed it) also vows to spend $500 million of its own on a competing system of wireless television in Latin America.

Under the group's charter, the three giants—Murdoch, Azcárraga and Marinho—have equal shares throughout most of Latin America. TCI holds a 10 percent share. Locally, though, it's a different game. Marinho has the upper hand in Brazil and no say in Mexico, while Azcárraga reigns supreme in Mexico but has no clout in Brazil. Murdoch is a minority shareholder in both Brazil and Mexico but, unlike his Latin partners, enjoys a crucial foothold everywhere in the region. What is more, Murdoch and Hughes both have other ways to make their wishes known—namely, fat bankrolls and arsenals of state-of-the-art technology.

Globo officials are confident that their foreign partners will not become predators and that national television stands only to gain from the foreign marriages. One of their insurance policies is local production. Indeed, some 85 percent of Globo's daily programming is produced in-house. Much of it comes from Projac, a colossal $60 million Hollywood-scale production villa on the outskirts of Rio, which turns out *telenovellas*, or serial films, featuring the country's best actors, writers and directors. Globo's four daily *telenovellas* dominate prime time. "We know that if the competition airs a foreign soap or movie at prime time, our *novellas* will beat them hands down," says Jorge Adib, Globo's director of international sales. Globo also sells $30 million worth of *telenovellas* a year to 70 countries.

Pay-TV has also helped create opportunities for independent producers. Once disdained by the networks, independents are finding an eager new customer in pay-TV. With the number of channels rising to triple figures, independents expect to increase their sales from $17 million in 1995 to $45 million this year. "The proliferation of channels means a bigger market and more competition, which can only help to raise the quality of television production to a higher common denominator," says Gabriel Priolli, director of TV Gazeta, a regional broadcast station in Sâo Paulo.

And what will happen when the grand old men of national media—Roberto Marinho is 91 and Civita is 59—pass the wand on to their sons and daughters? This older generation was the cornerstone of modern communications in Brazil, as Azcárraga was for Mexico and Cisneros for Venezuela. It was their courage and capital that took Latin American society from a world of grainy black-and-white images to that of direct-to-home satellite dishes. In many ways, their enterprises, by broadcasting from one end of the map to the other, helped unify entire nations. In Brazil, and especially at Globo, it will soon be time for the next of kin. But are Marinho's heirs, blessed with plenty and teethed in far tenderer conditions than the old man, up to the rigors of the new world of global television? There are probably as many answers as channels. For all their money and modern machinery, the foreign media giants—Murdoch and Hughes, Hearst and ABC—will need able local partners to deliver their magic to local audiences. Then again, men of Murdoch's mettle have made their fortunes at the edge, risking their shirts at times, navigating in the most perilous of realms—global communications.

The Marinhos and Civitas, by contrast, are smaller fry in these rugged waters. They have no maps, no familiar compass and, for the first time, no comfortable constitutional safety nets to fall back on. Long accustomed to dominating a closed and comfortable world of national broadcasting, they are now in the company of true giants. Today these companies are allies, but, at a time when the rules of communications are being torn up and remade, they can easily become tomorrow's rivals—mega-investors who have not only the teeth and talent but also a voracious appetite for new opportunities. Suddenly Latin America is a bowl full of angelfish, and the local species will have to swim hard or risk being swallowed.

Mac Margolis is a special correspondent for Newsweek *and a regular contributor to* The Economist *based in Rio de Janeiro.*

22

What Does It Taste Like?

Christina Scott

Malawi will gain its first television channel this June, courtesy of a deal struck with a Malaysian company. According to the postmaster-general in charge of introducing TV—outlawed until recently along with miniskirts and trousers on women—if he asked the average Malawian what he or she thought of TV, the answer would be, "What does it taste like?"

While other regions undergo merger mania, for the 500 million people living in Africa the biggest media issues tend to the basic: a supply of paper for the print media, windup radios with no operating costs, rechargeable car batteries for the television. A continent that has 12 percent of the world's population and 2 percent of its telephone lines cannot sustain much interest from Rupert Murdoch. In Africa, most media monopolies are still state monopolies. When interest from international media organizations appears in Africa, it is taken as a sign that economic conditions have improved to the point where freedom of information issues can be tackled. "Murdoch? We should be so lucky," was one comment.

For most people switching on a television somewhere between the Atlantic and the Indian Oceans, government broadcasts are by far the norm. And although several African countries are now flavor-of-the-year for the kind of high-risk international investors who were enamored of Mexico prior to the peso crisis, long-standing economic cleavages within each country mean that most people receive their information from state radio or, at best, from the BBC World Service.

South Africa is the only country on the continent to have attracted the attention of an international conglomerate—News Corp.—and even then, the attention is limited to buying certain screening rights. There is no investment in infrastructure as has been the case in Asian countries.

Nevertheless, out of Africa, always something new. In this case, the new is the growth of a homegrown media conglomerate, M-Net of South Africa (which also goes by the name of a subsidiary, Multichoice, and operates in Europe and parts of the Middle East as well), which has set up shop in the absence of much interest from the international players. Its presence around the continent is a measure of both the modest state of indigenous media industries and Africa's relationship to international media conglomerates.

M-Net was created in the dying years of apartheid rule as a decoder channel (the equivalent of pay-per-view in the absence of a cable network or a satellite transmission) for affluent South Africans. It used a terrestrial transmitter system owned and operated by the state broadcaster and was granted an hour of limited open time during which anybody with a television could watch. The consumer was compelled to buy a decoder from a shop, plus pay a monthly subscription fee—which was initially low but has outstripped inflation in what some pundits claim is an effort to shed TV-watchers whose disposable income does not impress the advertisers.

M-Net was funded to a large degree by English- and Afrikaans-language newspapers. No particular outcry about cross-media ownership was made; there were more pressing concerns. At present, inside South Africa, M-Net screens one current-affairs program a week, "Carte Blanche," which reflects the interests of its elite viewers in more than just the name: green issues, entertainment, human interest. An M-Net series interviewing senior political leaders required serious silliness: the interviewer, a popular satirist and female impersonator, wore more sequins than the Miss South Africa contestants.

However important M-Net may be in Africa, it is very much a junior partner when it stands alongside international conglomerates. M-Net paid $85 million to the multinational News Corp. to obtain rugby screening rights from Rupert Murdoch, who had negotiated with the South African Rugby and Football Union to obtain full rights to screen games—a deal that Minister of Sports Steve Tshwete desperately fought to prevent from happening. Rugby has long been a powerful symbol in South Africa—first of white domination and, since the 1995 World Cup victory, of racial reconciliation. But in the end, M-Net of South Africa had to negotiate with News Corp. to obtain screening rights to its own rugby matches.

Mvuso Mbebe, general manager of the National Sports Council, said: "We have to address the matter of top events being awarded to off-shore TV broadcasters, like the Rupert Murdoch rugby deal. There are certain sports events that we believe are public domain." Mbebe added that if a TV rights agreement with the sporting codes could not be reached, the South African government could step in and pass legislation to force certain events onto the public broadcaster.

In M-Net's business-minded outfit, the focus on entertainment, erotica and sport for upper-income viewers limits the station's appeal to elite audiences. The station's use of English means that M-Net will not become a power in Francophone Africa. Yet it probably would be a mistake to write off M-Net, the new kid on the conglomerate block, as a nonentity providing fantasies for expatriates, the families of deputy ministers and tourists in luxury hotels. If nothing else, its presence is a reminder that there are alternatives to state broadcasting.

The South African Broadcasting Corp., the state broadcaster, has renamed itself as a public broadcaster, retained its three national channels, started this year to report in 11 official languages, begun two regional TV breakaways and fallen under the control of the newly established Independent Broadcasting Authority. SABC news reporters are in an odd position because everybody is keenly aware of SABC's past as a mouthpiece. Criticize a minister and you are likely to be told that, as a lackey for the previous regime, you have no right to exercise common sense. Neglect a story and you are told that SABC is covering up for the new lot the same way it ignored the misdemeanors of the old. Ironically, the image of control is not based on financial needs: SABC covers its costs from license fees, advertising and cross-subsidization among channels. Digital and analog satellite equipment is now available, but the buyers seem mostly interested in sport, porn and entertainment from abroad.

Aside from the state broadcaster, the only other player is Bop TV, a station belonging to the former homeland of Bophutatswana. It has managed to survive through the guile of its newest manager, M-Nettrained Cawe Mahlati, and the fact that the broadcasting legislation was so badly drafted that the state is locked into continuing funding. Bop TV now delivers Tswana drama and English-language news and entertainment beamed at Soweto, the country's largest township.

However, black-owned Thebe Investment Corp. confirmed in March that its entertainment subsidiary, Moribo, was holding talks with an international television channel with a view to bargaining for a free-to-air television channel due to be launched next year. The project, called Station for the Nation, faces an expensive requirement for about 30 percent local content. And local content costs the equivalent of about $2,000 a minute to produce. (Imports, on the other hand, can be purchased for $200 a minute.) Station of the Nation has an advantage in its commercial alliance with one of the country's two film distributors, which will give expertise in negotiating film fights. The Thebe corporate communications staff, however, makes no mention of providing any news. Other competitors for the one license likely to be offered next year include a partnership between Kagiso Trust, a new black empowerment company, and Britain's Channel 4 television, or a partnership between the Youth Trust, a community organization, and Primedia, a commercial media organization.

South Africa's combination of a sprouting homegrown media conglomerate and continued state broadcasting might be beneficial. They give the country, and observers around the continent, time to see what influences could be wielded by multinational media organizations, and how to cope with those influences when, and if, those media organizations ever come to Africa. In the meantime, democracy has freed South African businesses to trade across the continent, and M-Net has moved into other countries—Nigeria, for example.

Nigeria has, in effect, two wings of state electronic media. This anomaly grew out of the civilian administration of President Shehu Shagari (1979–83). His party was not in power in all provinces, and those provinces that had minority parties in power demanded a structure of their own to provide a local mouthpiece as a counterpart to the national structure. The civilian administration has long since been replaced by a military government, but the state system continues side by side with the federal system.

Lagos, however, also has CNN, M-Net and the BBC. How do you define their impact? Although the majority of Nigerians live in rural areas, television is concentrated in the urban areas. If you believe in trickle-down theories, information of interest to the elite is eventually transmitted to the working class and the peasantry. On the other hand, in the early '90s, the Nigerian military dictatorship, in an attempt to keep out "cultural imperialism," asked CNN not to beam in, so we could operate on the assumption that any medium that irritates men in uniform and in power has the potential to be A Good Thing for Democracy.

In Nigeria, the national broadcasting commission has been issuing licenses for a small number of commercial radio and TV stations. RayPower 100, one of the new commercial radio stations, broadcasts news to Lagos. Its independence from the government is modest at best. I suspect that in West Africa, one of the better sources for understanding the society in which one lives is not the electronic news media—with the honorable exception of the BBC's World Service—or the print media, but allegorical plays and soap operas in the style of the late Ken Saro-Wiwa, the writer and leading advocate of the rights of the Ogoni people who was executed by a Nigerian military tribunal in November. Nigerian media professionals are not impressed with the changes in their country to encourage diversity and private ownership of media because the regulations governing the youngsters did not apply to that old granddaddy—the state. In other words, there was no leveling of the playing field.

Frustrated Nigerians might want to visit Nairobi, to play that old Monty Python game of "You think that's bad? That's nothing!" The postindependence Kenyan constitution enshrines the government—the Kenyan Broadcasting Corp. (KBC) radio stations and the Kenyan Television Network—as the only player in the electronic field of media. The government of President Daniel Arap Moi used this unsuccessfully to fight M-Net, which at present tends to be watched mostly by tourists in the seaside resort of Mombasa. CNN is also there. If homegrown or international media conglomerates ever lead the fight for press freedom in Africa, their first converts will be chambermaids.

Most Nairobi print journalists have not watched M-Net; still, those I spoke to welcomed it on the grounds that anything that made the government nervous had to have some redeeming qualities. Several quoted with irony the comment sniffed by the Kenyan Minister of Information and Broadcasting Ndolo Aya: "The concept of independent electronic broadcasting was ill-conceived."

The Kenyan government would consider this analysis unfair. A spokesperson pointed out that KBC subscribes to the BBC. Deutsche Welle is another official source of information. Radio Feba, which only produces religious programming, receives backing from churches to beam Faith to the Seychelles islands. The state has also established a media review panel, which is meant to regulate airwaves and award broadcast licenses. (A report from the panel is months overdue. If it has been released to the government, it most certainly has not gone any further.) Two private companies—with links to key state officials, it is said—received authorization in 1995 to own their own stations and produce programs. But the two companies, CTN Cable and Stellagraphics, seem to be in the mold of M-Net but without its resources or production values; their commitment is to money rather than to press freedom.

On a continent where freedom of expression is rare, Egypt sticks out for its own combination of problems. Like other African countries it is characterized by government control over information, the barest presence of media multinationals and the presence of M-Net. But the donor/diplomat two-step that put pressure on other countries like Nigeria and Kenya to diversify and divest is not present in Egypt because of fears among all concerned that Islamic fundamentalists will use a radio station or a TV channel to wage war on the Islamic moderates. In Egypt, pluralism in broadcast media is a remote prospect. There is a glimmer of hope in that the country's standard of living is higher than that of sub-Saharan Africa, so there are probably more families there who can afford satellite dishes.

If nothing else, the growth of satellite television in Africa, embodied by M-Net, has heralded an increasingly sophisticated offshore telecommunications infrastructure that will undercut governments' ability to intervene in communications. As a minor example, a proposal from the South African-based Telkom telephone monopoly to plant a fiber-optic cable around the continent triggered outrage from states who each already had their priorities in order: better to retain control over telephone lines and remain nations where business is stunted by their lack than have the economy grow without retaining control. Nonetheless, it looks like the cable circling the continent will become a reality, as each reluctant nation considered the possibility of its neighbors' economies outcompeting with superior access.

M-Net can attract the affluent portion of the TV-watching African public without enormous repercussions within the media world. Most state broadcasters do not screen ads, and so are unlikely to feel the pinch of migrating viewers. As M-Net grows, the possibility exists that the continent's media agenda will be set by business concerns located within southern Africa. News coverage may not even be on the agenda, pushed out by more profitable undertakings.

Still, M-Net's growth may free local industry of some government restraints. As Cheiok Tidiane N'diongue, director of Senegal telecommunications, notes, "To control the telecommunications sector in any country is controlling the totality of the economy, with security and defense taken out."

If satellite television, local or foreign, can take part of that telecommunications sector and make it independent, it has the potential to benefit the media industry, which now relies in every possible way on the ruling political parties. Perhaps M-Net will strike a glancing blow for press freedom without ever having screened a news bulletin.

Christina Scott is a radio and television producer for the South African Broadcasting Corp. She previously ran a news agency in Durban, which specialized in covering violence in KwaZulu/Natal province.

VII

Books

23

Megamedia Moguls and
Multimedia Madness

Anne Wells Branscomb

Commercial Culture: The Media System and the Public Interest
Leo Bogart. New York: Oxford University Press, 1995.

The Media Monopoly
Ben Bagdikian. Boston: Beacon Press, 1992.

Jihad vs. McWorld
Benjamin Barber. New York: Times Books, 1995.

Road Warriors: Dreams and Nightmares
Along the Information Highway
Daniel Burstein and David Kline. New York: Dutton, 1995.

Spreading the News: The American Postal
System from Franklin to Morse
Richard R. John. Cambridge: Harvard University Press, 1996.

Megamedia Shakeout: The Inside Story of the
Leaders and the Losers in the Exploding Communications Industry
Kevin Maney. New York: John Wiley & Sons, 1995.

We are rushing toward a digital world where hundreds or even
thousands of channels of information will be available in a variety of
formats. We are told that technology is placing more and more control

in the hands of users, who will determine what appears on their television screens and computers. Yet in our euphoria for such a diversity of choice, we often neglect to ask, What voice will consumers really have in who is going to program all of those channels?

Recent history offers few certain lessons. George Orwell's novel *1984* predicted a future of information centralized in the hands of a powerful elite, who would saturate the airwaves with powerful pabulum to turn those who listened and watched into malleable and obeisant worker bees. But the year 1984 came and went, and still we were neither malleable nor obeisant.

Computer pioneers envision a caring, sharing world in which we all sit at our personal computers and easily summon up all of the information in the digital world—a democratic, undisciplined but benign universe in which reason prevails. But these pioneers were themselves betrayed by one of their own, Bill Gates, who became the richest man in America by running a company that writes the software that controls a virtual world of personal computers. Still, in his book and accompanying CD-ROM, *The Road Ahead*, Gates pursues the dream that computer software will be a tool of personal freedom, not an instrument of slavery.

Where is this era of communications innovation, media empires and media mergers taking us? Where do the megamedia moguls fit in and what are their goals for us? Will they or we, either as consumers, as investors or as citizens, determine where the information superhighways will lead?

There is no lack of writers eager and willing to lead us in one direction or the other. Perhaps the most provocative book is Benjamin Barber's *Jihad vs. McWorld*. Barber describes a world in which two divergent forces are tugging in opposite directions. One force is that of the religious fundamentalists, who tear apart nation-states to create ever smaller communities that will better accommodate their diverse views. The other force is the global marketplace that weaves us all together into McLuhan's global village—a technologically controlled world of MTV music videos, McDonald's food chains and Macintosh computers. Barber argues that nation states are ill-equipped to deal with either trend. He recommends the return to what he calls "civic society," in which individuals deal with one another concerning public matters that they can only resolve collectively—something between an organized government bureaucracy, in which participation is only achieved through occasional votes, and a privatized corporate world (Barber seems to hold out some hope for the Internet as a worthy choice for development). However, he does not make clear how and whether megamedia corporate entities will control the gateways to these civic channels, and, if not, who will. Neither does he address the funding for such civic involvement in a world driven by advertising offered by private entrepreneurs.

Perhaps the most flamboyant and most readable book is Daniel Burstein and David Kline's *Road Warriors*, which argues that our civilization is at a historic turning point: either "government withers away, replaced by a global Internet-ocracy" or the mass media grows ever more powerful and transforms our court system into an entertainment circus that turns the entire world of watchers into a frenzied mass of O.J. doubters and devotees. (Do we really know the difference between news and entertainment anymore? And where do we turn to guard the integrity of fact?)

Burstein and Kline remind us that in the world of privatized and merged media there is still a role for government. After all, they recite, the Internet was jump started by government funding that has led to the current multimedia madness and a spurt of new information activities both public and private. Would we foreclose future seeding of entrepreneurial innovation by curtailing this source of funding, they ask?

More likely to help the gamblers than the philosophers amongst us to select which digital horse we'd like to put our money on is *Megamedia Shakeout* by Kevin Maney, a writer for the Money section of *USA Today*. He describes the world of megamedia as a horse race among the old giants and the new yearlings. He will more probably satisfy our yearning for personal profit from investing in the winners rather than the losers.

However, many of the companies that he touts as potential winners have already peaked in performance. In a period of intense experimentation, as much money may be lost as made, and predicting which may be which is a dangerous profession. One of his most promising companies, General Magic, has floundered on the stock market, although, to give Maney credit, he did say that General Magic "could make it big or not make it at all." And some companies seem to have taken Maney's advice, as when Disney acquired a television network to deliver its product and threw its hat into the ring of those who view the future as one of a few dominant companies with vertically integrated subsidiaries. That notwithstanding, Maney seems to contradict his own advice to Disney by warning that vertical integration could fizzle because content providers will want as wide a distribution system as can possibly be devised. At stake are two different visions of the future of our media. The model of a competitive information marketplace offers a multiplicity of sources of message generation, all bubbling in a cauldron from which everyone may ladle out their choice serving. The vertically integrated model, however, conjures up entities controlling both content generation and distribution.

Media moguls' mergers in the world of television and motion pictures reflect an assumption that bigger and more integrated media organizations are likely to be more successful. The digital world, however, is a far more complex, ever-changing and confusing place. It reveals a different set of assumptions. Yesterday's behemoths, IBM and ATT, are downsizing, and some minuscule start-ups on a shoestring are outperforming these old stars. A representative of a tiny start-up confided to me recently that its only competitor was IBM. Yet the start-up already had 100 percent of the business in its tiny but lucrative market niche. This does not necessarily mean that small start-ups are the wave of the future. While the more innovative strategies and products often emerge from entrepreneurs acting outside large bureaucracies, as these smaller companies become more successful (many of them do not survive infancy), they seek to be acquired by the larger companies with greater financial and marketing resources, thus completing the cycle of innovation and absorption.

For example, US West recently acquired Continental Cablevision, making the CEO of this privately held but third-largest U.S. cable company the newest billionaire. Amos "Bud" Hostetter declared that the reason he turned to US West, rather than a public offering, was that he saw the handwriting on the wall and that a merger would be far more successful than going it alone in the new global marketplace.

Maney appeals to our desire to profit from the digital revolution, not our hope to understand what it all means philosophically. He shows no sign of the angst that plagues both Benjamin and the Burstein/Kline team. Maney's confidence in the technology and ebullience over its success is overwhelming. The only unknowns are which companies and media moguls will reach the pot of gold at the end of the rainbow or, alternatively, land at the bottom of the digital dumping ground.

Maney concludes with a sweeping hurrah for U.S. technical expertise and business acumen: "On the world's playing field megamedia could take the United States somewhere almost beyond imagination." Maney sees U.S. brand names dominating the global marketplace in both software and transmission capability. But this view may be myopic to the extent that it does not take into consideration major acquisitions of U.S. information-based companies by European and Asian interests and the trend toward mergers into global conglomerates. Moreover it ignores the backlash that is represented in Barber's Jihad and the less hostile, but nonetheless strong, concern emanating from Europe and Canada about U.S. cultural imperialism. It may be that "beyond imagination" can be good or bad, or both good and bad, but as yet unforeseen. Maney remains a writer clearly focused on CEOs of Fortune 500 companies, investment capitalists and the investors that fund young entrepreneurial companies. His appeal is to our pocketbooks, not our civic-mindedness.

This book is a far cry from Leo Bogart's *Commercial Culture: The Media System and the Public Interest.* Bogart's analysis, contrary to Maney's, delves into the realities of how U.S. media are financed and for what purposes, and how they affect international media. At the hearings for the 1934 Communications Act, moguls of radio made high-minded statements about how they would pursue the "public interest" and never permit the medium to be dominated by advertising. Today, however, almost every major communications medium is dominated by advertising. It is hard to remember that promise of then-Secretary of Commerce Herbert Hoover, who said of radio: "It is inconceivable that we should allow so great a possibility for service, for news, for entertainment, for education, to be drowned in advertising chatter." The transformation of this once new and great medium for public service into a megamedia machine for the generation of advertising dollars and commercial exploitation is a warning to all those who believe that the new media are immune to commercial excesses.

Bogart's book deserves careful reading not only for its litany of the problems of the past, but also for its historical account of policy measures—Fairness Doctrine, minority ownership, affirmative action—directed toward assuring that the media serve "the public interest" rather than the mere whims of its owners or the entertainment choices of its listeners and viewers. Bogart's prescriptions for current develop-

..it in public policy are particularly pertinent. He offers a wealth of choices for consideration, especially with regard to issues that are not subject to resolution through balancing the books on corporate assets. His proposals range from eliminating complacency about media violence through relentless publicity concerning its harmful effects to recognizing communications channels as public utilities and separating carriage of messages from control over the content of the messages transmitted. Bogart's book is a plea to examine of where we are headed with the convergence of media before we reach the point of no return.

Are we abdicating our responsibility for self-government to the megamedia moguls who aggregate us into audiences for advertising in support of a consumer-oriented economy? It is their right to freedom of speech that the First Amendment protects, and the courts have consistently, with a few exceptions, held that individuals have no right of access to the media. Is there a "public interest" to be pursued through the megamedia products? And, if so, which public or publics does it serve? Burstein and Kline observe that in 1993, Mitchell Kapor, then chairman of the Electronic Frontier Foundation, which is dedicated to the preservation of fundamental freedoms in electronic communication, was looked upon as a "party pooper" when he asserted at a gathering of media moguls that "we are not just consumers; we are also citizens!"

As regards our citizenship, Ben Bagdikian, in his ground-breaking work *The Media Monopoly*, issued an early alert in 1983 about the dangers of concentration of media ownership: "To give citizens a choice in ideas and information is to give them a choice in politics; if a nation has narrowly controlled information, it will soon have narrowly controlled politics." Yet Bagdikian's warning about the chilling effects of media concentration and the influence of advertising over content seems to have fallen on deaf ears. Nothing seems to have changed in the decade since he concluded, "Today the integrity of news and other public ideas depends upon corporate self-control, on the hope that the large corporations that now control the media will not use that power as an instrument to shape society to their liking."

If we as consumers choose to rely upon corporate self-control as the sole arbiter of content, we must be mindful that the First Amendment provides greater protection to those who control the corporate gateways than to those who seek access to their media facilities. A major problem is the way that the First Amendment protects owners of media outlets and prohibits interference by outsiders (either government or individuals or groups) with content. While owners may assert their First Amendment rights to speak as they like, the First Amendment does not guarantee access to individuals. But the First Amendment was based upon the assumption that there would be many publishers, that they would speak their many minds and that such a cacophony of diverse voices would compete for the support of the populace. As the number of media owners who control access to information transport systems diminishes, the rationale for guaranteeing them free reign to control both the means of transmission and the content transmitted becomes questionable. It is appropriate to remember A.J. Liebling's famous remark, "Freedom of the press is guaranteed only to those who own one." Can that be translated today to a protection of those who own personal computers or those who own the networks interconnecting those personal computers?

Long before multimedia sprang upon the stage, this conundrum was one of the major reasons for establishing the common-carrier concept for transmission of messages in the postal, telegraphic and telephonic sectors. Common carriers are obligated to accept all comers without prejudice and without any legal liability for the content. Publishers, on the other hand, not only pick and choose what they wish to publish—they are legally responsible for what they publish.

The importance of the common-carrier concept is clear in Richard R. John's historical analysis. *Spreading the News* provides an important explanation of the role of the federally supported postal service as an agent of social change, which unified a diverse population of colonists into an integrated and powerful nation-state. John describes how a passive cash cow linking major commercial centers, employing 75 percent of federal workers and supplying a major source of federal income brought news of the centers to the hinterlands and bound the previously separate colonies into the world's greatest democratically governed nation. Today, the postal service has been minimized to that of only one of many alternative ways of transmitting information around the country. Indeed, the postal service has been prevented from offering electronic alternatives to physical delivery of mail, thus hampering its capability to offer a modern version of the full-service "information highway" that it provided in the 19th century.

We are entering a new era in which private companies acting in their own self-interest individually are expected collectively to perform a function that has been for the last 200 years performed through a government mandated system. It is interesting to note that the USPS has itself become a slave to the advertising of direct mail marketers. Thus, it is no less driven by commercial concerns than other media.

At the same time, the common carriers are seeking to become information providers rather than mere conduits of content provided by others. As telephone companies become information providers and the opportunity to discriminate against other information providers increases, the telephone companies cannot have it both ways. The cable companies have always been a hybrid—required to carry local broadcasters and required to make some channels available for lease but able to program some of the channels themselves. However, the efforts of Ted Turner, annoyed because some of the limited channel systems were not carrying his CNN or TBS, led to court decisions breaking open the mandatory carriage rules This eliminated some public broadcasting stations from the local line-up and extended more First Amendment privileges to the cable companies to exert greater control over content on their systems.

If these trends continue with fewer and fewer companies competing to provide content, and even fewer bound by a commitment to accept all comers, then the goal of a vigorous "marketplace of ideas" may be in jeopardy. Before such a scenario should come to pass, it behooves thoughtful citizens to consider how access to the megamedia moguls can be achieved.

Now, with everybody entering everybody else's market, legalized and encouraged by the new Telecommunications Act, it is virtually impossible to determine who should be a common carrier required to accept all comers and who should be a publisher entitled to monarchical control over content issued in its name. The question may become moot if the megamedia moguls become so intertwined with mergers and joint ventures that we cannot discern one from the other. Indeed, one sometimes wonders if the only way to assure universal access to content for media outlets is to maintain a state-owned and managed system that legally could not discriminate against any content provider under the First Amendment. This, of course, is not likely to occur, as the anti-government sentiment is widespread, not merely domestically but internationally.

In this time of media mergers and communications conglomerates, the Internet—a loosely interconnected network of networks where each node operates independently without any centralized governing body— may be the most promising medium of communication that we can devise to maintain diversity of content, not only for U.S. residents but for users worldwide. Perhaps the Internet will provide an opportunity for small groups, even individuals, to sustain unfiltered access to the marketplace of ideas without going through a screening process directed by an advertiser-influenced conglomerate or a media mogul with his own views about politics and morality to be urged upon the world.

Yet even if cyberspace is expandable, the attention span of viewers is not. If we have turned the courtroom into a multimedia zoo, the road to the White House into a backbiting road show of negative advertising, our homes into movie theaters, our shopping malls into frenzies of home-shopping channels and Web pages and our offices into cocoons of telecommuting isolation, will there be a public space where we can discuss and resolve the problems and issues that plague us?

All these books give us ideas to help us work our way through the technological wonders, the myriad media companies and the men who are leading us into this "brave new world" with either our active participation or passive consent. The hyperbole and apprehension in their pages indicate that most of us do not have the foggiest idea where we are going, and those who think they do may be completely wrong. What is certain, however, is that those that stand on the sidelines and watch will not have a role in determining where the information superhighways go and what they will find when they get there.

When the dreamers dream of a utopian future, they paint a picture of each of us at our "comsole" (a mixture of computer, television and multimedia libraries that Maney calls the "computophonovision"), plugged into a world of information that will supply us with whatever we need for our health needs, our education, our entertainment, our financial security and our religious preferences. But many of us abdicate our individual responsibility as citizens to participate in deciding how these needs will be met other than by an "invisible hand" guided by our consumer interests and advertising dollars. That is the direction in which we seem to be going. Perhaps we forget that the institutions that have served us in the past are a rich mixture of consumer-supported businesses, tax-supported governmental agencies and nonprofit entities supported either by our dollar contributions or our investment of time and personal energies. If our worst nightmares come back to haunt us or our utopian fantasies become realities, we will have only ourselves, not the megamedia moguls, to blame or to thank.

The late Anne Wells Branscomb, a Media Studies Center inaugural fellow, was a professor at Harvard University's Program on Information Resources Policy and a communications attorney. She is author of Who Owns Information? From Privacy to Public Access *and editor of* Toward a Law of Global Communications Networks.

For Further Reading

Alleyne, Mark D. *International Power and International Communication*. New York: St. Martin's Press, 1995.

Auletta, Ken. *Three Blind Mice: How the TV Networks Lost Their Way*. New York: Random House, 1991.

Bagdikian, Ben. *The Media Monopoly*. 4th ed. Boston: Beacon Press, 1992.

Barnet, Richard J., and John Cavanagh. *Global Dreams: Imperial Corporations and the New World Order*. New York: Simon & Schuster, 1994.

Bogart, Leo. *Commercial Culture: The Media System and the Public Interest*. New York: Oxford University Press, 1995.

Brunn, Stanley D., and Thomas R. Leinbach, eds. *Collapsing Space and Time: Geographic Aspects of Communication and Information*. New York: HarperCollins, 1991.

Burstein, Daniel, and David Kline. *Road Warriors: Dreams and Nightmares Along the Information Highway*. New York: Dutton, 1995.

Clurman, Richard M. *To the End of Time: The Seduction and Conquest of a Media Empire*. New York: Simon & Schuster, 1992.

Drake, William J., ed. *The New Information Infrastructure: Strategies for U.S. Policy*. New York: The Twentieth Century Fund Press, 1995.

Dunnett, Peter J.S. *The World Television Industry: An Economic Analysis*. New York: Routledge, 1990.

Flower, Joe. *Prince of the Magic Kingdom: Michael Eisner and the Re-making of Disney*. New York: John Wiley & Sons, 1991.

Goldberg, Robert. *Citizen Turner: The Wild Rise of an American Tycoon.* New York: Harcourt Brace, 1995.

MacLeod, Vicki, ed. *Media Ownership and Control in the Age of Convergence.* London: International Institute of Communications, 1996.

Maier, Thomas. *Newhouse: All the Glitter, Power, and Glory of America's Richest Media Empire and the Secretive Man Behind It.* New York: St. Martin's Press, 1994.

Manes, Stephen, and Paul Andrews. *Gates: How Microsoft's Mogul Reinvented an Industry—and Made Himself the Richest Man in America.* New York: Simon & Schuster, 1993.

Maney, Kevin. *Megamedia Shakeout: The Inside Story of the Leaders and the Losers in the Exploding Communications Industry.* New York: John Wiley & Sons, 1995.

McManus, John H. *Market-Driven Journalism: Let the Citizen Beware?* Thousand Oaks, Calif.: Sage, 1994.

McPhail, Thomas L. *Electronic Colonialism: The Future of International Broadcasting and Communication.* Newbury Park, Calif.: Sage, 1987.

Nordenstreng, Kaarle, and Herbert I. Schiller, eds. *Beyond National Sovereignty: International Communication in the 1990s.* Norwood, N.J.: Ablex Publishing Corp., 1993.

Picard, Robert G. *Media Economics: Concepts and Issues.* Newbury Park, Calif.: Sage, 1989.

Pilati, Antonio. *Media Industry in Europe.* London: John Libbey, 1993.

Pines, Burton Yale. *Out of Focus: Network Television and the American Economy.* Washington: Regnery, 1994.

Salvaggio, Jerry L. *The Information Society: Economic, Social, and Structural Issues.* Hillsdale, N.J.: Lawrence Erlbaum Associates, 1989.

Sapolsky, Harvey M., Rhonda Crane, W. Russell Neuman and Eli M. Noam, eds. *The Telecommunications Revolution: Past, Present and Future.* London: Routledge, 1992.

Schiller, Herbert I. *Culture, Inc.: The Corporate Takeover of Public Expression.* New York: Oxford University Press, 1989.

Shawcross, William. *Murdoch.* New York: Simon & Schuster, 1992.

Smith, Anthony. The Age of Behemoths: *The Globalization of Mass Media Firms.* New York: Priority Press, 1991.

_____. *The Geopolitics of Information: How Western Culture Dominates the World.* New York: Oxford University Press, 1980.

Steinbock, Dan. *Triumph and Erosion in the American Media and Entertainment Industries.* Westport, Conn.: Quorum, 1995.

Stevenson, Robert L. *Communication, Development, and the Third World: The Global Politics of Information.* White Plains, N.Y.: Longman, 1988.

Thomas, Dana Lee. *The Media Moguls: From Joseph Pulitzer to William S. Paley: Their Lives and Boisterous Times.* New York: Putnam, 1981.

Tunstall, Jeremy, and Michael Palmer. *Media Moguls.* London: Routledge, 1991.

Turow, Joseph. *Media Systems in Society: Understanding Industries, Strategies and Power.* New York: Longman, 1992.

U.S. Department of Commerce. *Globalization of the Mass Media.* Washington: U.S. Department of Commerce, 1993.

Wriston, Walter B. *The Twilight of Sovereignty: How the Information Revolution Is Transforming Our World.* New York: Charles Scribner's Sons, 1992.

Index